Social
Phobia

Social Phobia

From Shyness to Stage Fright

John R. Marshall, M.D.

with the assistance of Suzanne Lipsett

BasicBooks

A Division of HarperCollins*Publishers*

Designed by John Chung

Library of Congress Cataloging-in-Publication Data

Marshall, John R., 1939–
  Social phobia : from shyness to stage fright / by John R. Marshall; with the assistance of Suzanne Lipsett.
      p. cm.
  Includes bibliographical references and index.
  ISBN 0–465–07214–3
  1. Social phobia. I. Lipsett, Suzanne. II. Title.
RC552.S62M37 1994
616.85'22—dc20   93–45449
                                                                              CIP

---

94 95 96 97 ❖/RRD 9 8 7 6 5 4 3 2 1

For my parents,
my wife, Kathleen,
my children, Brent and Erin,
and all my patients

All the world's a stage.
—SHAKESPEARE

Contents

Acknowledgments

I would especially like to acknowledge the substantial contribution of Suzanne Lipsett. More than just writing and editing, her thoughtful questions and challenges pushed me to speculate and draw meaning from clinical experiences beyond my cautious academic stance. I am also grateful to Darci Feggestad, who did the lion's share of the work and especially for her constant cheerful attitude in keeping up with my many changes. I am also grateful to Donna Littel and Jen Meuli, the other women of module D6, who chipped in to help me meet deadlines. A special thanks is due to Ned Kalin, my good friend and colleague, for his encouragement to begin the book and above all to continue, and finally a special thanks to my patients who have taught me so much and make psychiatry so rewarding.

Prologue:
The Disorders of the Decade

About ten years ago, a colleague of mine asked me to assist him in running an anxiety disorders clinic in the Department of Psychiatry at the University of Wisconsin, in Madison, where I taught. I am a general psychiatrist and professor, and up to that point most of my clinical teaching and research had been focused on what is called consultation-liaison psychiatry. This subspecialty, dealing primarily with the relationship between medical illness and psychiatric conditions or symptoms, is exciting and often dramatic. I worked with very sick patients—for example, people on dialysis units or organ-transplant recipients—and was often challenged to sort through their medical and psychiatric histories to track the origins of bizarre and mysterious symptoms. Needless to say, the work was continually engaging, and I was not entirely sure I wanted to add anything more to my professional plate. Besides, anxiety-related conditions had never been a major focus of psychiatry, and I had not had much clinical experience.

Not that anxiety was unknown in my work—it was ever present for psychiatric patients, and cropped up constantly in their descriptions of symptoms. Anxiety manifested itself in a range of ways—sweating, nausea, increased heart and breathing rates, agitated thinking, shaky hands, weakness in the joints, sleeplessness, and even chest pains and constriction that mimicked heart attacks. But my training had conditioned me to consider anxiety itself a *symptom*—the effect of some other condition rather than a condition in itself. Whenever patients reported anxiety, the practice of the time was to search for conscious and/or unconscious conflicts related to childhood experiences that might be causing it. So the traditional orientation actually deflected psychiatrists' attention *away* from anxiety, encouraging us to ignore or look past someone's painful, often disabling feelings and symptoms.

In retrospect, I realize that we were so preoccupied with trying to divine the "real meaning" of anxiety in Freudian terms that we failed to hear much of what our patients told us about what was really troubling them. And in our search for an underlying problem, we gave short shrift to the extreme discomfort that anxiety, in all its physical and psychological manifestations, caused.

At about that time, a great many articles on anxiety began to appear in scientific journals, many written by people I regarded highly. Increasingly, in the early 1980s, anxiety disorders emerged as psychiatric conditions in their own right, and reports began surfacing on two ways of treating them: either pharmacologically or with cognitive and behavioral therapies. (The latter are newly developed therapies that focus on changing thoughts [cognitions] or specific behaviors.) The idea of developing a clinic—a separate, personalized unit within a large, sometimes faceless institution—began to attract me, and as I read extensively, my attitude toward anxiety began to change. Perhaps anxiety did deserve a fresh look; perhaps, in my search for "the cause" and "the answer," I was moving too quickly past my patients' reports of anxiety and its ravages on their lives. My second thoughts were echoed in the literature at large. Collectively, psychiatrists were coming to admit to a blind spot where chronic anxiety was concerned.

I accepted my colleague's invitation, and soon our clinic was attracting people from all around the region. We designed research projects of our own, and the clinical pictures of anxiety gradually began to sort themselves out. I started hearing the same stories in response to my questions over and over, the same patterns of disabling fears. Gradually, as a range of discrete anxiety disorders began to be described in the literature, I found that I could recognize a particular disorder for what it was, rather than seeing it as a murky clue to be followed into the unconscious. And, gratifyingly, as I learned how to treat anxiety disorders, I began to see rapid, sometimes dramatic, improvements in people whose self-esteem had been deeply eroded by lifelong battles with often bizarre fears, people who had been helpless at understanding or finding a way out of what was happening to them, people who had been hopeless about ever enjoying anxiety-free lives with the pleasures and enrichments that others took for granted.

Now, this was something of a novelty for me. As a general therapist, I was not all that accustomed to seeing people get better. In the process of traditional insight-oriented psychotherapy, my patients and I would usually eventually agree on "the cause" of the problems that brought them into therapy. But some symptoms would almost always persist or seemed to follow an almost random course. Now we know that some conditions, including anxiety disorders, are not caused by unconscious conflict or symbolic processes; for these problems, even determined, prolonged efforts to discover "causes" are doomed to failure. And yet, with the newly emerging treatments my anxiety patients were making remarkable turnarounds. These apparent cures, along with the burgeoning research into anxiety disorders, combined to keep me fascinated and excited and renewed my commitment to my profession.

My own optimism was mirrored in the mental health community. At about the same time, major advances focusing on the central nervous system in genetics, biology, ethology, physiology, and pharmacology had broken down interdisciplinary barriers, allowing a broader, more penetrating look at anxiety-related symptoms and behavior. These developments led to the creation of reliable criteria for diagnosing anxiety disorders, giving us a language with which to communicate about these conditions. By 1980, the *Diagnostic Statistical Manual of Mental Disorders,* published by the American Psychiatric Association and used by most mental health professionals, contained new, precise descriptions of anxiety disorders clearly distinguished from other psychiatric illnesses; the 1987 revised edition added further information. Clinicians were now able to recognize, test for, and treat anxiety disorders more easily and with more certainty than ever before.[1]

In 1980, the National Institutes of Mental Health conducted intensive epidemiologic surveys to assess the extent of mental health problems in the United States.[2] This remarkably comprehensive house-to-house survey conducted by trained interviewers in four major American cities had amazing results. The findings reassured me that I had committed myself to work that was meaningful and significant. The 1980 survey showed that anxiety disorders were the most common psychiatric conditions in the United States: 8.3 percent of the population suffers from an anxiety disorder during any six-month period.

These results countered expectations among mental health workers. Most of us had believed that "affective" disorders—disorders of mood such as depression and mania—topped the list in the United States. Not only were anxiety disorders most prevalent, they were also confirmed by other researchers to be the reason most people sought help from mental health professionals.

General practitioners may not have been as surprised as psychiatrists by these findings. They had long been aware that anxiety-related symptoms played a major role in motivating patients to seek help and in causing symptoms that defy diagnosis or treatment. One large study found that 11 percent of all patients came to their physicians with anxiety as their chief complaint.[3] Other studies suggested that from 12 to 31 percent of medical doctors' patients suffered from "severe anxiety."[4]

This new understanding about anxiety disorders has allowed clinicians to give up old, narrowly conceived theoretical biases and adopt models of syndromes that are more easily testable and more clinically effective. The result has been a flood of interest so strong that psychiatric clinicians and researchers came to refer to the 1980s as "the decade of anxiety." Researchers identified and developed treatments for a wide range of discrete conditions, from simple phobias to panic disorder, from obsessive-compulsive behavior to post-traumatic stress and generalized anxiety disorder. (For a description of the other known anxiety disorders besides social phobias, the focus of this book, see the appendix.)

My initial reluctance to become involved with the anxiety clinic evaporated completely as I worked with patients and watched them progress in their treatments. In the past I had had a discomfiting sense of starting from scratch with each new patient, but now the medications and therapies coming into use had reassuring confirmation in laboratory science. Even more rewarding was the experience of being someone's last resort—a last resort that *worked*. Many of the people who came to us had undergone years of psychotherapy to no avail; often they felt hopeless, resigned to living lives severely impaired by their unexplained fears and anxiety. Yet with a combination of pharmacologic and specific cognitive and behavioral treatments, the word *cure* seemed entirely appropriate.

We saw a full range of anxiety disorders in the clinic, but gradually I began to take a special interest in a set of quiet patients who, by the very nature of their disorder, kept a low profile and presented a less flashy array of symptoms. Some of these individuals would have been described by most laypeople as extremely shy; indeed, the psychological literature of an earlier, more poetic time referred to them as "morbidly shy." But there is more to this disorder than mere social reticence—their terror of social interaction and its consequences is as intense and debilitating as that of people under siege or threat of physical attack. The intensity of their fear of human encounter is comparable to the reactions of a phobic person at the sight of a snake.

Perhaps in part because of my own memories of painful social encounters as an adolescent, I was increasingly drawn to these patients. Their diagnosis, social phobia, was a subtle but intensely disabling form of anxiety, a form that often made it impossible for the person to take comfort in the company of others. I found this condition particularly cruel—a virtual formula for loneliness, despair, and failure. Throughout the 1980s, I worked with many socially phobic people and experienced, along with them, exhilaration at their responses to treatments that were proving to be effective. During that time I came to realize how often social phobia goes unrecognized and thus untreated. It was for that reason that I decided to write this book.

Chapter 1

Buried Secrets/Buried Lives:
Two Case Histories

E VERY PSYCHIATRIST DREADS the suicidal patient. Although the young woman who entered my office on this particular day did not relate a typical tale of depression and despair that signaled a potential suicide, she nevertheless admitted—in a voice barely above a whisper—that she had twice come near to killing herself. She was twenty-nine years old, a brilliant physics student. Later, after I had succeeded in gaining her trust, she would tell me that she had stolen a beaker of cyanide from one of the university labs. She kept it in a closet in her room and planned to drink it if her life continued on as it had been.

Telling me these things was clearly a nightmare for Julie. She kept her eyes downcast, riveted on her hands, which squeezed each other tightly. She simply could not look at me during our first few sessions. Her voice was tremulous and I had to interrupt repeatedly to tell her I could not hear her.

In a later session, after she was able to relax with me, she told me that coming into the clinic had been one of the hardest things she had ever done in her life. This came as no surprise to me—distress was evident in her voice, her face, and her posture. What was not evident, what I had to imagine, was the courage it took to keep her appointment.

This is Julie's story, pieced together from her sessions with me:

"I was always the shy one in my family—a bookworm. I read all the time in my room upstairs—everybody else always sat around together downstairs. On holidays especially, my parents were always trying to get me to join them, but I just wanted to dive into science books. I dreaded those holidays more than anything. When I think back on high school now, I can see myself getting more and more self-conscious, more and more buried in my work. It used to be I'd try to dig into my work and make the outside world disappear. But at some point it changed, and it was me I was trying to make disappear.

"By the time I entered college I had figured out how to do that—I lived in a room in a quiet family's house and worked all the time. I never went anywhere except to my room or the lab. It wasn't until I had almost graduated that I found out how other people saw me—I was 'brilliant,' 'eccentric,' 'a born scientist.'

"I knew they were all wrong. I was just horribly, horribly self-conscious. I cut class whenever I could, and even talking to my professors and my landlord, the only people I couldn't avoid, was an ordeal—I knew they'd see how scared I was and know how wrong they'd been about me. I kind of liked knowing everyone thought I was so smart, but I was sure the minute they heard me talk they'd think I was just a dishrag, a fraud, and not so brilliant, kind of stupid. Cold, shaky hands. Transparent skin—look! You can see my veins!"

Julie would glance up briefly, but generally she looked down or leaned her ear against the chair back and laid her arm across her eyes. It was a way, long ingrained, of avoiding eye contact.

"In graduate school, people started hearing about my work. It began to look as if I could really make a contribution to my field, and my professors hinted that they had high expectations for me. Pretty soon, all I had to do to get my degree was make an oral presentation in a course I had already dropped because I couldn't make myself get up in front of the class. The thing was, I knew there was no way I was going to be able to do it without making a total fool of myself. I kept putting it off and putting it off, but the more I waited the more scared I got. Soon I started worrying not just about stuttering and blushing in front of the class. I was afraid I'd vomit, right there in front of them all."

This was a dramatic revelation. It was easy to see that expressing the thought was emotionally agitating for Julie.

"Once this thought occurred to me, I couldn't get rid of it. The scene played itself over and over and over like a movie loop: of me standing in front of the whole class, with the professor there who I respected so tremendously and who wanted me to do so well . . . and being sick on the floor.

"After that, I don't know . . . I just can't understand it. The thought just terrified me. I knew it was just a thought, but I'd go into a cold sweat whenever it crossed my mind. I really think the idea of me getting sick in front of all those people was starting to drive me insane."

When I met Julie, she had almost quit trying to control her imagination and "talk some sense" into herself; she had finally admitted defeat. Only desperation and the fear that she was going crazy over this "little problem" made it possible for her to seek help at our clinic. The one thing she feared more than coming in and talking to strangers about herself was going to a mental hospital.

"It's crazy. I know I'm letting my whole career, my whole *life*, go down the drain. I love my work and I'm good at it. My project has been finished for a year and a half—other academics have even written requesting the results. I've practiced my presentation hundreds of times. I could make it in my sleep to an empty room. But—"

"But—?"

"I can't do it," she whispered, as she had many, many times. "I feel like such an idiot. Such a fool. But I'm too afraid to do it."

There was no mistaking Julie's desperation. Not only her future as a scientist but her physical existence was threatened; she spent many hours in a darkened room, beaten down by depression over what she called her "chickening out."

I recognized Julie as one of a group of clinic patients whom most people would classify as intensely shy. And I felt a particular empathy for her, as I remembered my own shyness. My family and peers would have been surprised to know how much I struggled to appear at ease—and although I succeeded, and participated in athletics and school activities, everything Julie and patients like her described was familiar to me in kind if not in degree.

The experiences of an older man, a successful neurologist, increased my fascination and made me more optimistic about treating cases like Julie's. David was fifty-five, with a private practice in a small Midwestern city. Unlike Julie, David was able to look me straight in the eye; his professional demeanor was evident even in his role as patient. In fact, it would have been difficult for most people to imagine David having even a moment of self-consciousness.

Initially, he sought help at the clinic for insomnia. When he explained that episodes of sleeplessness occurred only on Wednesday and Thursday nights, I asked him to describe the usual sequence of events that might account for the fact that he had trouble sleeping on those particular nights.

"Well—" he began. "It's my wife's dinner parties at the country club. On Fridays."

"Yes?"

He remained silent for a moment and then blurted out, "Yes. Those damned dinner parties." His professional demeanor crumbled. "They scare me to death."

After a deep breath, he elaborated. "My wife seems to think it's a crime to stay home on the weekends. Every Friday night she has something lined up for us to do—dinner with this couple, dinner with that couple, we owe them one, they owe us one. . . . I don't know. I just can't stand it. I don't remember when it started exactly, but I started worrying about these things coming up every Friday at the country club. We never entertain at home. I just have to be able to leave . . . "

"And do you stay home?"

"No, no. So far I've managed to make myself go—but the

worry! It's ruining my practice. I'm walking around like a zombie all the time."

"What, precisely, has you worried?"

After another long silence, he answered in a weak voice, "I'm afraid I won't know how to act."

He told me how his anxiety escalated throughout the week in anticipation of the Friday dinner party. On Wednesday evenings, he became tense. Calming himself with several drinks before bedtime, he would sleep only fitfully. On Thursdays he would be more anxious and completely unable to sleep that night. On Fridays he felt "nearly incapacitated," partly from exhaustion but mostly from anticipation of the evening's events. For the past three months, fearful of his agitation being noticed, he had refused to schedule patients on Friday afternoons and secluded himself with medical record dictations.

On Friday evenings, although he would "fortify" himself with several substantial drinks before leaving for the country club—straight from his office—on several occasions he had to stop at home to change his shirt, which had become soaked by perspiration. He endured the meals, he said, in a haze of self-consciousness. His bewilderment was evident as he cataloged his fears to me. Unlike Julie, he seemed relieved to be speaking of a secret that had been plaguing and disturbing him for some time.

"I don't know what it is. I have no problem at the office talking with patients or the people who work for me. I'm fine on the phone with other physicians. But at those damned dinners I'm just terrified of saying or doing something embarrassing—"

"Something like what?"

"Like spilling something, tripping, even choking on my food. I'm just afraid I'll make a tremendous fool of myself. I sweat, tremble, flush. To try to keep things under control, I order very little food and just sort of push it around on my plate—I can't eat. With each bite I think the food is going to go down the wrong way, and just can't stand the idea of choking and coughing and turning red while everybody's just sitting there, paralyzed, staring at me, and seeing my face all contorted . . . "

With a variety of excuses, David and his wife usually left the club early. "Then I'm safe for another week. Once at home I feel pretty comfortable, and at work, as long as I can 'act like a doctor,' I'm perfectly okay."

I asked him whether he had felt at ease in social situations as a teenager and young man.

"Oh, I was always uncomfortable with people. I haven't given a speech or any kind of talk since high school, but still, that works out okay. On a one-on-one basis in my practice, I think I'm pretty good. As long as I'm in control, I mean."

The standard definition of social phobia matched Julie and David's problems: "A persistent fear of one or more situations . . . in which the person is exposed to possible scrutiny by others and fears that he or she may do something or act in a way that will be humiliating or embarrassing."[1] After diagnosing Julie and David as social phobics, I began to devise plans to help them using new treatments that combined psychotherapy with drugs.

NEW HOPE FOR THE "NEGLECTED DISORDER"

Real hope emerged in 1985 for people like Julie and David, when the psychiatrist and researcher Michael Liebowitz and colleagues Jack Gorman, Abby Fyer, and Donald Klein drew attention to social phobia as the "neglected disorder" in a landmark paper in the *Archives of General Psychiatry*.[2] In response to that paper, other scientists began studying the condition and an array of effective treatments started to surface. Now, great numbers of people— probably about 2 percent of the U.S. population, or 5 million individuals, many long considered to be "morbidly shy" and virtually untreatable (although treatment was seldom tried) are able to find help in entering the world of social interaction fully and even with pleasure.

The new understanding of anxiety disorders and the trend in psychiatry toward melding pharmacological and psychotherapeutic treatments have been highly effective for anxiety disorders in general and social phobias in particular. But the challenge remains: how to reach those hundreds of thousands of socially phobic people who are unaware that they suffer from a *treatable condition* and who remain hidden away, avoiding all social contact. The chapters that follow are meant to convey life-changing information to those who need it most, people who experience severe social anxiety—what we have come to call "social phobia"—those who care about them, and mental health workers who care for them.

SOCIAL PHOBIAS

Socially phobic patients express the same central concerns. Simply stated, they fear that they will make fools of themselves in public. Of course, all of us share this concern to some degree and occasional social anxiety is normal. But the intensity, duration, and disabling effects of their deep fear of humiliation distinguish real social phobia from shyness. Men and women appear to be equally affected, although males are more likely to seek help than females. This probably reflects the fact that in our society men are still more likely to hold positions in the workforce that exacerbate social fears; this factor may change as other social patterns change. Middle- and upper-class patients are more likely to seek help, although all social classes are affected. As for racial distinctions, although we know that the disorder crosses racial and ethnic boundaries, clear statistics are not yet available.

Social phobia commonly arises in early adolescence, although there is much variation among individuals. Some describe themselves socially anxious throughout most of their lives, while others believe that their symptoms originated only in later life. Most sufferers first seek help in their late twenties or early thirties, usually when they reach a critical point in an occupation, profession, or in their hopes for a relationship or family.

There are two categories of social phobia—*circumscribed*, or *specific*, social phobia and more *generalized* social phobia, like

Julie's. In the specific form, exemplified by David's fears, anxiety is elicited by certain situations—dinner parties, eating in public—and generally does not arise in other social arenas. For many people, though, this diagnostic distinction is blurred.

The most common specific social phobia is the fear of speaking or performing in front of a group, known as *performance anxiety*. Again, most people initially experience a certain amount of nervousness about such situations, but they are still able to perform satisfactorily. Furthermore, the anticipatory anxiety leading up to the presentation generally abates as soon as the individual begins to speak or perform. For the phobic person with this fear, however, the terror is intense and all-consuming long *before* the actual performance and unremitting *during* it. And the fear neither abates as the event proceeds nor does it wane in subsequent performances.

Above all, the person with performance anxiety is terrified of humiliation—of being evaluated and judged negatively by the audience. Commonly, the person believes that he or she will show signs of anxiety such as choking, blushing, or sweating—in Julie's case, vomiting—and that such signs will heighten one's embarrassment to the point of making the performance intolerable. So horrible is the possibility of failure that the person can only hope to gather the strength to bolt and run. Contrary to common belief, such dread of embarrassment is surprisingly common among professional performers and can become a significant and painful impediment to their careers.

Other specific social phobias concern drinking or eating in public (for fear that one's hands or head will shake visibly or that swallowing will cause choking), writing in public (out of fear that the hand might tremble, revealing one's anxiety), and urinating in public restrooms (for fear of being heard or observed).

Other specific social anxieties covered in this book arise not only in the workplace and the world at large but at home and in the bedroom at large.

People like Julie, who have generalized social phobia, may

experience some or all of the particular fears just discussed, but they also fear meeting new people in *any* context, formal or casual. They are particularly anxious in encounters with "authorities" or with members of the opposite sex. To protect themselves against painful experiences, they adopt behaviors of deferral, avoidance (often by silence), withdrawal, and escape.

Because these sufferers worry that others might notice their physiological fear responses, such as blushing and trembling, they become excruciatingly self-conscious. They are usually inwardly focused, convinced that others think critically of them; they are viewed as extremely shy by others. Not surprisingly, confidence and self-esteem are notably low, and over time they may become deeply lonely, hopeless, and depressed. Many people who enter treatment for specific phobias are found to be suffering from these more generalized social fears.

HAPPY ENDINGS

It is gratifying to report that both Julie and David responded dramatically to treatment at our clinic. David improved with remarkable speed on a medication called phenelzine (a drug therapy discussed in detail in chapter 10). David and I also met several times to examine his fears and to devise behavioral techniques to allow confrontation of the dining situation.

Julie, after several sessions in which we explored the nature of her fears, agreed that it made sense to focus on the special performance situation she had been unable to face: the oral presentation needed for her degree. First, I prescribed and taught her how to use a beta blocker medication, atenolol, which inhibits the physical symptoms of anxiety. Second, we spent several sessions exploring Julie's catastrophic cognitions: those thoughts, common among social phobics, in which a situation's worst possible outcome is envisioned (this will be discussed in more depth later). At each step we dealt with the realities of her fears. For example, we discussed the likelihood of people actually thinking she was a failure if they noticed her anxiety—given that the sort of presentation she faced was difficult for almost everybody. Also, after years of contact with her and their familiarity with her work, would her professors actually think less of her if she were to stumble, "say the wrong thing," or even become ill and vomit? Finally, the behavior therapists in our clinic arranged for staff members and patients to form an audience before whom Julie could practice. In this situation, she was able to experience the positive effect of medication. Her relief at the blocking of her physical symptoms—and the realization that her body would no longer betray her by revealing inner turmoil—actually made these sessions enjoyable for Julie, even when the "audience" pretend to mutter derogatory comments. After several of these trial runs, Julie made the much feared presentation to her class with no difficulty. She told us that within fifteen minutes of beginning she actually found herself feeling exhilarated. Julie's last visit to me was a celebration of her triumph. "You know, you really were my last resort," she told me. "If I hadn't been able to finish that course, there would have been no point for me to go on living."

Chapter 2

The Evolutionary Origins of Social Anxiety

Fear is a vital evolutionary legacy that leads an organism to avoid threat and has obvious survival value.

—Isaac M. Marks, 1987

I WAS GRATIFIED by the improvements my socially phobic patients experienced, but increasingly it seemed important to try to understand *why* drug treatments, often used in combination with specific psychotherapies, were so effective, particularly in cases where psychotherapy or psychoanalysis alone had no effect. Actually, it is common in medicine for effective treatments to emerge for conditions that are themselves poorly understood. And frequently such treatments can help to provide information about the underlying disease mechanisms. In the case of social phobia, the particular drugs that proved during the 1980s to be useful affected neurotransmitter mechanisms that facilitate the movement of nerve impulses throughout the nervous system. This observation strongly suggested the possibility that social fears and behaviors were somehow ancient, inherited mechanisms "built into" human physiology. And this line of thinking led to consideration of the "hard wiring" of the human

psyche to explain why in socially phobic people these mechanisms have become intensified to a disabling degree. In an
attempt to trace the roots of these intensified responses back to
the bases of human mentality, we have to ask some fundamental
questions about the place of fear in our species.

NORMAL VERSUS ABNORMAL ANXIETY

The subjective term *fear* covers a wide range of specific responses.
Fear is a normal response to real danger. In no uncertain terms,
it is a lifesaver: fear is the set of survival responses that galvanizes
us to face life-threatening challenges. But in the group of psychological phenomena known as anxiety disorders, sufferers react
with intense fear to situations where there *is* no objective source
of bodily danger such as a predator or a fire or, in more abstract
terms, a life-threatening disease. In these cases, we call the subjective experience of these fearful symptoms *anxiety*.

Of course, many forms of anxiety are normal and even useful. For example, anxiety surrounding a public presentation can
motivate us to work hard to excel—in the effort to assuage our
anxious feelings we may actually succeed more completely than
if we approached an impending presentation with a casual confidence. Most people can relate to the anxiety that accompanies
the steady descent of one's bank balance—without going into
the symbolism of money as a means of survival, we can view anxiety as an uncomfortable reminder of our responsibility to
reverse the direction of the numbers. For many people, attain-
ing financial security is as much an effort to eliminate the symptoms of anxiety as it is a matter of money.

But these normal manifestations of anxiety are distinct from
the symptoms of the anxiety disorders. To be considered a discrete disorder, anxiety symptoms need to occur *in excess*, to cause
significant distress, and to interrupt normal functioning. In
patients with anxiety disorders, the traditional distinction between
fear and anxiety becomes blurred. In situations that most people

would not consider realistically dangerous, anxiety patients react with all the fear responses described earlier. In effect, the disorder is a heightened sensitivity to, or an overactivation of, the internal defense system. The alarm may be just as loud, just as agitating, and just as demanding as in the case of real danger. For the sufferer of an anxiety disorder, the repeated alarms bring normal life to a halt and, until a mechanism is found for turning it off, they absorb the individual's full attention.

THE DANCE OF SURVIVAL

The question of how or why our internal defense systems might go awry takes us to prehistory and human evolution. Our biological defense or safety systems have evolved to protect against injury or attack. These systems have different components having to do with attention, evaluation, feelings, and behavior, and in primates and humans they are highly complex.

Scholars believe that there are three levels of the defense systems. The first is a *nonsocial defense*, which evolved primarily to facilitate defense against predators. This state is marked by very rapid startle responses, hyperalertness, quick discharges of behavior, and movements that make rapid flight possible. This quick-acting short-term capability, designed to create behaviors that permit the escape from predators, exists in all animals who are subject to predation.[1] Many researchers consider phobias, panic disorder, and agoraphobia to be remnants of this original system in humans.

The second level of defense that evolved is called the *territorial* system. This system regulates social organization *within* a species and is quite prominent in birds, reptiles, and solitary mammals. Its central expression is the obtaining and guarding of a home base. The animal uses display behavior to attract potential mates to its territory. Concurrently, potential mates gather to engage in intersexual displays (for example, birds may show plumage and members of the same sex have competitive encounters). In this system, an animal of either sex establishes on the basis of its ability to "hold" or secure, resources. (Female birds, jackals, lions, and many others appear to engage in territorial struggles.) The animals show plumage, perform mating dances, clash antlers, posture, or vocalize to "strut their stuff." An individual's ability to maintain his or her territory is called resource-holding potential.[2]

What makes this system work is another evolutionary development: the animals' capacity to *evaluate* the resource-holding potential of others of their species; compare this to an estimate of their own relative capabilities; and make a decision, estimate, or evaluation on the likely outcome if a serious fight ensues. Without this ability to evaluate the competency of the other with regard to oneself, carnage and the eventual destruction of the species would ensue. In fact, it is rare for animals within a species to injure one another fatally.

The third development in the safety system is the *group-living* level, a subsystem that evolved from the others. This higher system—found in group-forming mammals such as primates and humans—is the capability of signaling submissiveness, appeasement, and subservience to a more dominant individual. To send these signals, an animal must have a hypersensitivity to signals of power and must be constantly ready either to challenge or to send appeasement signals. These behaviors permit the individual to stay within the group rather than being driven away, as occurs in more primitive territory model.

HIERARCHIES FOR GROUP LIVING

The evolution of the group-living system made it possible for individuals to live together in relative peace. True groups could evolve as a result of the development of a social hierarchy: a "social submissive system" with social *fear* at one end of the spectrum and social *dominance* at the other. Every single individual in the group, male and female, then took its remarkably precise place along the continuum from dominant to submissive.

To preserve or adjust the social order of a group, dominant individuals retain their position by having antagonistic encounters with other members of the group. Dominance hierarchies are most often male, but not always. In some species, the females have their own dominance hierarchies parallel to the male system. And at least in the case of velvet monkeys, females dominate the males and have their own hierarchies.

Within the group, animals try to convey information about their strength and courage in subtle, often highly complex signs and signals that frequently are unique to the species. Among primates, whose social hierarchies have been studied in depth, facial expression and particularly movements involving the eyes play a major role in these encounters. So, for example, a dominant male chimpanzee might stand erect and fix opponents with wide-open, staring eyes under frowning brows. If the opponent returns the expression in kind, with similar self-confidence and aggressiveness, the first must decide whether to risk combat or signal submissiveness. The repertoire of submissive signaling behaviors varies from species to species. In primates it includes gaze avoidance, crouching, "fear grimacing" (which is very like an appeasing smile in humans), and so on. Carl Sagan and Ann Druyan have explained these complex systems in their book *Shadows of Forgotten Ancestors: A Search for Who We Are.*[3]

Such signaling does more than save the weaker animal from a dangerous fight. By appeasing the dominant animal, the weaker individual gains the opportunity to stay with the group rather than being driven out into a potentially dangerous environment to fend for him- or herself. This yielding is distinguished sharply from "giving up" and "losing." The animal that submits and appeases by no means becomes defeated, withdrawn, and depressed. Rather, this individual remains highly attentive, in constant physiological arousal and hypersensitive to the dominant individual, ever ready to signal further submissiveness should the need arise.

Perhaps the most relevant component in this system of social positioning is the role of facial expressions and their dual meaning as communicating signals. In very practical terms, grimaces, smiles, and the shifting of gazes tell the threatener that he or she has won, that there is no need to continue the harassing display. But facial expressions, as well as submissive postures, also convey a second meaning: they signal that the individual is experiencing a complex emotional state, a subtle and disturbing orchestration of subjective feelings and physiological reactions that we call, collectively, *fear*.

SOCIAL FEAR IN HUMANS

Scientists who have focused on the evolutionary development of social anxiety in humans hypothesize that, just as in other primate species, social anxiety in humans has developed as part of our group-living system and has become part of our genetic endowment. And, again as in other complex species, anxiety around other people helps us assess the likelihood and degree of threat or dominance that others represent and allows us to live peacefully together, maintaining a fine balance of aggression and inhibition. In a small but telling example, consider the sixth-grader who comes home complaining, "I *hate* Ms. Anderson. She *looks* at me." "She *looks* at you?" respond the parents. "You mean she yells at you?" "Nope," replies the boy. "She never yells. She just nails you with her eyes and you know you're in trouble." Educators seeking methods of controlling twenty or thirty unruly twelve-year-olds have long relied on "the look" to inspire anxiety leading to subordination in their young charges.

It is important to note that human social behaviors have complex systems of motivators besides defensive ones designed to protect. Here we are focusing on these defense systems because they relate to anxiety mechanisms, but humans also have caring, reassuring "safety" systems that lead to and reinforce attachment between members of the social group. These systems include parent/infant bonds; cooperative endeavors; mutually reassuring signaling such as holding, hugging, kissing, greeting; intricate networks of etiquette and politeness; apologizing; complimenting; taking turns; and other socially reciprocal behaviors.[4] Like lions that rub muzzle to muzzle within their prides, we have our habits of shaking hands or embracing and kissing at the door. We may experience them as spontaneous expressions of affection, but these behaviors are actually complex greeting and leave-taking rituals that contribute to the coherence of the group.

All these systems represent highly evolved modes of social interaction. When they fail to inspire a sense of safety and security—or conversely when threat is perceived—more primitive or defensive systems come into play. Researchers believe that, possibly because of genetic influences or environmental experience, socially anxious people overemphasize the dominance/submissive mode, becoming "stuck" in this view of the world and unable to participate in the cooperative, mutually reassuring safety systems.

Socially overanxious people tend to misinterpret others' behavior as displays of power or competence and respond with behaviors that signal submission. Thus, they freeze, inhibit their own spontaneous interactions, cringe, crouch, smile appeasingly, and anxiously attend and try to please. Eventually, these highly strung individuals seek relief from their own constant hypersensitivity to social signaling by withdrawing. By this point, though, their unrelenting focus on what they perceive as their weakness relative to others has culminated in generalized social phobia. In this context, this journal entry written by a twenty-eight-year-old male admissions counselor takes on an evolutionary significance:

"I'm always thinking and worrying about how strong I am. I feel great, and that makes me feel like a real strong person, and then somebody says some little thing or looks at me in a certain way, and I'm a wimp. At school especially, I'm just a wimp—I'm overly polite, I'm overly apologetic. Just a total fool. Some days on campus I go through an entire day and the only words I say

the whole time are 'I'm sorry' or 'excuse me.' Why do I go over-
board trying to please people? I never know whether I'm strong
or weak. I never know how to act."

FEAR OF REJECTION

Although our society is becoming more violent and dangerous,
our laws still function to preserve us from attack against life and
limb. Furthermore, though by no means perfect and in many
cases highly imperfect, our complex system of resource alloca-
tion does result in some sharing of the wealth. (Where it does
not and sustenance is threatened, the level of anxiety suffered is
certain to be very high.) What precisely is it, then, that people
with extreme social anxiety fear? What is it that is so frightening
nowadays?

One compelling answer is that humans' fundamental fear is
based on a primitive dread of *rejection,* resulting in abandonment
by the group. As I noted earlier, being banished from one's
primitive social group—whether monkeys, chimpanzees, or
human beings—to fend for oneself all alone in a potentially dangerous environment once indisputably threatened one's survival: banishment could lead to death. It is not surprising, then,
that social phobics often feel—irrationally, they admit—that the
social circumstances they fear have life-or-death meaning. Fears
of criticism or disapproval, of being deemed of low social worth
and thus rejected, become fears of banishment.

Although socially phobic patients suffer extreme anxiety in
many different situations, all these circumstances generally
involve self-presentation to status-threatening others, comparisons and self-evaluation, and the possibility of a major loss in
status. Speech giving, job interviews, work-related meetings, parties, introductions to "important strangers," oral exams—in all
these situations, although we are generally unaware of it, we are
all jockeying for position or risking our present status in the
human social hierarchy.

For example, I asked Tom, a twenty-two-year-old who came to our clinic, what sort of a person he had the most difficulty being introduced to. "It's strange," he replied. "They are usually male and seem to have the characteristics I most want. They look strong, they're good looking, they appear very self-confident. I really feel okay around people I consider to be nobodies—I can even joke, I can make small talk, all the kinds of things I wish I could do on my job, where it would really count. But if I'm introduced to someone I really respect, or somebody I'd like to *be*, I can't even look them in the eye. I'm particularly worried that they will notice my hands are sweating. And I'm completely frustrated, because I can't be myself in front of them. I just can't relax."

Tom was completely unaware of the underlying meaning of his difficulties. He was comparing his own strengths and weaknesses with the men he encountered and involuntarily signaling submissiveness to those he judged stronger than himself. As is also characteristic of the socially phobic, "courting" situations also stimulated in Tom similar concerns about failure, loss of status, and banishment from the group. "The really cool guys always get the women," said Tom. "So who's going to be left for me?" An ethologist might view this as a dramatic vocalization of concern over competition for limited resources.

THREAT SITUATIONS

What happens in situations that trigger anxiety in social phobics, for example, being called on in class, being watched (and presumably evaluated) while one works or eats, or any social event where people stand around and talk while they "look each other up and down"? Let us follow Tom into a meeting in the ad agency where he works. In this particular meeting, the five account managers are to update their projects for the creative vice-president, as they do every Monday morning. During the first half hour, before each account manager presents a report on his projects, the men stand around and drink coffee. Among animals, this might be seen as an opportunity for display behavior.

"I almost feel I could make my presentation more easily if I didn't have to do this coffee-and-donut thing," Tom says. "I don't dare come in late—I think the other guys would notice, and wonder why I wasn't there. But just trying to chat and laugh and listen to these other cool guys standing around shooting the breeze sends me into a cold sweat. By the time it's my turn to report on my accounts I'm in my total wimp phase."

Very socially anxious people have lower expectations for success in social situations than most of us, and are prone to slip into the dominance/submission mentality whenever they find themselves in the presence of others. Their heightened vulnerability to negative appraisal causes them to be hypervigilant. Thus, the night before such a meeting, Tom begins to worry about what the other account managers are thinking about him. And as soon as he enters the conference room he hunts for clues in their faces and eyes. This is the equivalent of a subordinate primate reassuring himself that the dominant animal is not angry or threatening.

In this highly anxious state, any perception Tom might have that he is failing in other's eyes, or any suspected criticism of his behavior, appearance, or presentation, triggers a collapse of whatever confidence he might have been able to maintain. He becomes doubtful of his own capabilities and sure that he is "overmatched" by everyone in the room. This wave of doubt in turn triggers an array of submissive and appeasing behaviors not unlike that seen among primates in the wild:

- Avoidance of eye contact. "I know I should look them straight in the eye, but I just can't make myself do it."
- Flattening of his voice tone. "It's so frustrating. I know I'm droning, but I seem to have lost control of my voice."
- Inability to speak up and project. "Everybody in the room has this kind of hearty, confident way of talking, but people are always yelling at me, 'What was that, Tom?' or 'Could you speak up,' which only makes things worse."

- Curved, head-drooping body posture. "I always have a backache when I leave these meetings. One day, in the men's room along with two or three of the other managers, I caught sight of myself in the mirror. I looked like a goddamn question mark."
- Habitual apologies and self-denigrating statements. "Whenever I get the courage to try to make a joke, I notice it's at my own expense. They laugh like hell at each other's jokes, but when I make some remark they look at me with a kind of smiling pity, like they don't know what to say."

A lifetime of this sort of hyperalertness to his own inability to function socially had transformed some of these responses into permanent parts of Tom's presentation to the world, or even, some would say, of his personality. Even without the external triggers—the actual signals others sent to him regarding their relative strength—Tom's anxiety became the air he breathed.

It is important to emphasize that these behaviors—the vigilance, appraisal, comparison, and the resulting submissive behaviors—do not function as such within the realm of consciousness. As Sagan and Druyan point out, preprogrammed behavior that is part of our genetic makeup occurs in a narrow margin between "knowing" and "running on automatic pilot." Within this "thin partition," they argue, "the instruction in the genes is often in more control than the wisdom in the brain."[5] In cognitive therapy, in which self-reflection and reason are brought to bear on one's underlying thoughts and assumptions, part of the effort is to make patients aware of the effect of preprogrammed tendencies and its biological purpose.

But what happens when the submissive behaviors triggered by hypervigilance to evaluation fail to "work" in ensuring the person his or her place in the group? Tom sought our help because he was certain that his anxiety was clear to everyone in the room, that it was making him look like "a total fool" to his peers. It was all he could do to make himself attend these meetings in order to keep his job. As the moment approached for his own presentation, he could hardly remain seated at the table. In fact, on several occasions he bolted, later claiming sickness, and he knew he would not be able to pull that off many more times.

The urge to bolt has specific meaning in the struggle to remain in the social order. We have discussed the dangers of leaving the group for animals in the wild. If in humans the "civilized" submissive responses fail to bring reassurance of acceptance, less highly evolved anxiety responses—escape, fighting, freezing, or some mixture of all three—come into play, albeit involuntarily.

Making matters even worse, these behaviors are often accompanied by a flood of autonomic symptoms: accelerated breathing, increased heart rate, sweating, muscle tension, trembling, blushing, and other physical manifestations of anxiety. These are precisely the symptoms that socially phobic patients name as unbearable and, once they occur, as greatly intensifying their discomfort. This is because, once they perceive these responses in themselves, the symptoms perpetuate the condition by "proving" to the individual as well as to observers that he or she is weak.

Do these symptoms or behaviors actually succeed in ensuring the safety of the anxious signaler? Ironically, there is evidence to suggest that subservient, fearful, "cowering" behaviors among humans actually *increase* the likelihood that stronger individuals will attack. Although Tom believed that his co-workers accepted him rather benignly as a "wimp" or just simply "uncool," many of my patients have suggested that others find them annoying, disgusting, and even hateful.

Although far from verified in the research, the possible backfiring of submissive behaviors in this way, which might elicit attacks from stronger members of the group, could explain a great many puzzles in the history of human cruelty. For example, one study of schoolchildren in the 1960s found that an aggressive child was more likely to repeat an attack on another if the victimized child showed defeat, submission, or even injury.[6] Accordingly, self-defense classes counsel students to walk with head up, with a firm gait, showing alertness and a sense of purpose in order to avoid attracting aggression.

THE IMPOSSIBLE DREAM

In the presence of others, socially phobic people are generally *chronically* in a state of hypersensitive readiness to respond to threat or status uncertainty. The vigilant search for cues of relative strength and weakness requires a constant psychological and physiological readiness to fend off attack or flee. This state is so steady, and its symbolic relation to survival so fundamental, that it drives everything else from the psychic landscape—including the ability to enjoy the company of others, to banter, to speak one's thoughts with ease, to empathize with others, sometimes even to hear what others have to say. When a person's entire being is straining to catch every subtle signal, relaxing and taking pleasure in the company of others becomes an impossible dream. Not only every encounter but the *anticipation* of every encounter triggers the biological responses to a physical threat. The myriad ways in which those responses are expressed in the daily lives of social phobia sufferers are the subject of the next chapter.

Chapter 3

The Drama of Social Phobia

His servants disregard him. His very friendships wound him. He loses the object of his affection because he is too bashful to woo.
—E. Bulwer-Lytton, 1863

OF ALL THE SOCIAL FEARS, one of the most frequently cited by patients in surveys is "being introduced to a stranger."[1] For the socially fearful, each introduction to a new person is a highly charged test situation filled with self-conscious evaluation and monitoring—in primitive terms, assessing the others' comparative resource-holding ability. To the outside observer, the person may be managing this ritual with relative ease, but inside rages a torrent of maddening questions:

- What is this new person thinking of me?
- How am I coming across?
- Am I doing anything unusual, embarrassing, ridiculous, awkward—anything that will leave me open to criticism or even ridicule?
- Are my hands sweating?
- Is my grasp firm enough—or is the person repelled by that damp, dead-fish sort of handshake you hear people talk about with such disgust?

- Did I shake hands long enough?
- Did I shake hands too long?
- Did I look the person in the eye?
- Was my gaze too direct?
- Should I have broken eye contact sooner?
- What on earth am I supposed to say next?
- What will we talk about when the introduction is over?
- Who is supposed to begin the conversation after the introduction is over?
- What did he say his name was? What if I have to introduce him to somebody else? I can't remember his name!

These nervous, answerless questions fill every social moment of my patients' lives. And all these questions stem from a hypersensitivity to scrutiny. Outside the circle of safety that their own homes usually represent, these people are unable to forget for even a second that they are being observed, judged, evaluated by others. So burdensome is this awareness that many of them become virtually housebound. A vast array of behavioral patterns helps them avoid or minimize meetings with others. Here is a sampling of the strategies they devise:

- "I can't walk anywhere," says one man. "I always drive, no matter how short the distance, because walking down the street or crossing the street and facing oncoming pedestrians is just a torture to me."
- "I can walk on the sidewalk if I keep my eyes down, but I'll go far out of my way to avoid the line for a movie theater. Once, I turned a corner and found myself facing a line outside a door waiting for the unemployment office to open, and I thought I'd faint," reported a young, attractive woman. "All those men looking at me. I knew they were talking about me as I went by and that they'd all start laughing as soon as I reached the end of the line. I crossed right over a busy four-lane street. I know the people in cars were looking at me and they started to honk when I stepped out into the street. But at least I couldn't *see* or hear them watching me. I thought I'd die of humiliation from that, and I've never walked down that street again."

- "I never go out during the day. Nighttime helps, but I'm really most comfortable in the fog."
- "When my car started giving me trouble—that's when I stopped going out. The possibility that it would break down and people passing would see me standing there like a fool, and I'd have to deal with the tow truck guy and then the mechanic—it was just too intimidating. I consider myself a nondriver now, and I find that it's a relief. I don't have to worry about what people might think of me when they see me on the streets or after we ha· some sort of exchange."
- One woman told me that she was unable to turn left on a busy street. "If I make any turns at all, they are right turns." This mystified me. What did it have to do with her social anxiety? "I can't stand the idea of holding up other people either in my lane or in the oncoming lane of traffic. I can see in my rear-view mirror or in their faces as they wait that they think I'm an idiot, a horrible driver, a coward. I just can't take their criticism, especially when it's combined with honking."

After listening to hundreds of descriptions of "what could happen" to humiliate my patients, I have come to recognize various common categories of threatening social experiences, each of which has the potential to become, in the mind of the sufferer, an unforgettable minidrama that makes "next time" even harder to face. The following sections describe some common occasions that evoke great trepidation for socially anxious people.

"I HATE TO SHOP"

Contributing to the humiliation involved in social phobia is the banality of the fear-inspiring situation. While the wider world interprets courage in grand terms, many socially phobic patients must garner their deepest resources merely to go shopping at the corner store or—even more daunting—a supermarket or department store.

In part, dread of shopping exacerbates general distress at

being watched or meeting someone in the mall or store that one might have to talk to. However, more specific fears are also involved. One woman describes the difficulty she has browsing in a store. "I'm so self-conscious I often don't even see what I'm looking at. I'll be drawn to a counter by something I want to check out and then start worrying so much about what I'll have to say to the salesperson that I completely forget what it was that caught my eye."

I asked this woman to try to elaborate on her feeling—was she afraid the salesperson would criticize her choice, or ask her to move on?

"It's almost as if I've done something wrong—as if I've shoplifted, a thing I've never even contemplated in my life, and am about to be confronted. I'm always expecting or imagining the person behind the counter to demand that I just figure out what I want and stop wasting their time."

Another woman told me, "It's very hard for me to say, 'I'm just looking. Please let me browse.' I'm always afraid of offending people who have a job to do. And if the salesperson is pushy or aggressive, it's very hard for me to say no. Often, they'll force me to make a choice between two items I really don't care for. I find myself in a position of putting clothes on hold that I have no intention of returning to buy. Or sometimes I actually buy things knowing I'm going to have my mother return them, just because I can't say no to the salesperson."

"What *precisely* is it that you fear?" I asked.

"I'm always afraid I'm going to hurt the person's feelings or make them mad at me."

But it is not an overdeveloped sense of empathy that accounts for the social phobic's inability to assert him- or herself. It is the humiliating possibility of being thought ill of or being perceived as unreasonable or uncooperative. Over and over, my patients have repeated this same refrain: "I'd rather die than suddenly become the center of attention." Here again is heard the underlying ancient fear of scrutiny by group members and the anticipation of a negative response by them.

After listening to hundreds of descriptions of patients' terror of shopping and making purchases, I have come to wonder whether successful salespeople actually sense and use this fear to zero in on socially anxious customers, exerting pressure to buy. Many of my patients dread above all having to make large purchases, such as cars or computers, and often ask others to shop with or for them. I must admit I consider it a wise idea, since it avoids the risk of getting fleeced and humiliated all in the same exchange. For people in treatment for social phobia who are learning and practicing assertiveness skills, I urge them to start small, entering and browsing in unthreatening stores for minor goods.

WRITING IN PUBLIC

Martin was a forty-year-old executive whose job required that he make numerous presentations to colleagues and customers using an overhead projector. He was always very nervous before and during these presentations, but his focus of attention became his hands.

Would they shake? He knew they would, and that as he made notations that were projected onto the screen for the audience, the tremors would be magnified to the point where they would become the focus of the audience's attention as well as his own. This possibility kept Martin from sleeping on nights before his presentations. Although no one had ever mentioned the tremors—it seemed probable that no one else noticed them at all—one day he became overwhelmed by anxiety at this possibility and rushed from the room. Leaving the projector on, he fled the building, leaving the audience far more puzzled and perhaps annoyed than they might have been at the notice of his hand tremors. Shortly afterward, Martin made inquiries about entering treatment at our anxiety clinic, hoping for some kind of explanation to explain this mysterious inner plague on his sense of social ease.

It seems unlikely that we could ease Martin's trepidation by citing the ancient, evolutionary fears of showing weakness while engaging in displays before potential dominants or critics, but remembering our biological nature helps to explain Martin's seemingly baseless agitation.

The fear of writing in the presence of others is a common symptom of social phobia. A National Institutes of Mental Health study published in 1991 found this to be the third most common fear among its socially phobic subjects.[2] And a 1988 survey of social fears in the greater St. Louis area found that 2.8 percent of the population shared this problem.[3] Anxiety about writing before others appears to be part of a larger fear—that of performing tasks under scrutiny. But writing is an especially difficult act to perform in public, because it requires fine motor skills and is therefore highly sensitive to changes in grip or pressure caused by muscle tension.

Specifically, at the root of this phobia is the fear that observers will see the writer shaking, scribbling, or scrawling; that one might not be able to form the letters; or that one will "freeze" and be unable to complete the task. These specific anxieties quickly lead to by now familiar catastrophic thinking: "The observer will notice and think I'm ridiculous, incompetent, a fool and an idiot."

Most commonly, our patients first notice their fear of writing while in checkout lines at stores. The impatience—or the perceived impatience—of those in line behind them seems to heighten the sense of "performance." One young professional woman related an almost tragicomic incident that occurred in the checkout line at her supermarket. She had been acutely aware of an attractive man directly behind her in line, and as she wrote a check for her purchases a drop of mucus fell from her nose onto the check she was writing. Although no one else seemed to notice it, the idea that the man behind her *might* have seen it not only horrified her but initiated a full-blown fear of writing in public places. She was unable to complete writing the check and, until she sought treatment, completely unable to write in public again.

The inability to write in public may sound like a slight impediment, something that is easy to avoid. But it actually causes many constrictions in patients' lives, ranging from minor inconveniences to major challenges, especially at work, where it is often manifested as an inability to use a keyboard of any kind. When we consider that this fear rules out writing on blackboards in front of groups and signing credit cards and checks, we begin to grasp the scope of the problem. Renting cars, staying in hotels, signing in and out of ᵥrious activities, applying for loans, and signing documents or contracts all become difficult or impossible. Often, the more important the transaction, the greater is the anxiety. Official papers requiring a witnessed signature become a major threat to the sufferer's psychological and even economic well-being.

TELEPHONE PHOBIA

Most of us give no thought to picking up the telephone to make or receive a call. Even someone familiar with social phobia and its debilitating intensity might presume that the relative anonymity and lack of face-to-face contact would make telephone transactions far less threatening than other forms of social contact.

I was made acutely aware of the difficulties in one of my first experiences years ago on a radio call-in show where I had been invited to discuss social phobia. On the air, I remarked that I was surprised, and even a little disappointed, that most of the people who called in seemed to have anxiety-related disorders other than social phobia. On my next day in the clinic, one of my socially phobic patients told me she had heard me on the radio. "And if others are like me, there is no way you could have expected them to call in. I would never *dream* of calling in to a radio program. That would only multiply my chances of making a complete fool of myself—astronomically."

Chastened, I began to inquire more carefully about phone

behaviors. Many of my patients confessed that they avoided using the phone whenever possible.

But why? I would ask. What exactly do you fear about these encounters?

The several expressed fears were remarkably consistent. First, they worried that they would fail to make the appropriate response—they felt suddenly uncertain whether some special rule might have escaped their attention. After all, telephone rituals are probably far more difficult to learn through imitation than face-to-face behaviors, since children *and* adults rarely have the opportunity to listen to both sides of someone else's phone conversation. Socially anxious people fret, "Am I doing something inappropriate that the person will notice?"

Others feared that, because they would not know what to say, embarrassing silences would ensue and at the point when the conversation falters, anxiety would cause their voices to change, quiver, or squeak. They were terrified that they might stammer, stutter, or in other embarrassing ways give evidence of their disturbed state. The underlying concern of inadvertently conveying a sign of weakness is evident.

Many of my patients who reported these difficulties said they pressed others in the home to answer their calls. Knowing the identity of the caller and the topic of the call enables some preparation, much preferable to "being caught off guard with nothing to say." For those with this fear, answering machines and voice mail have been godsends. Conversely, the possibility of visual communications, whereby you and your caller see video images of each other, is unlikely to find enthusiastic support among socially phobic consumers.

As one might expect, there is a hierarchy of difficulty related to phone calls. People with social phobia can often handle routine inquiries that require answers to single questions, but casual or informal conversations that are likely to be prolonged or move in unanticipated directions cause much more difficulty. And of course calls that could involve evaluation—for example, with bosses, teachers, lawyers, potential dates, and so on—are the most stressful. One woman had no trouble with any of these types of calls, unless someone else was in the room watching her talk. This variation would have her quaking with the fear of evaluation by the witness to her conversation, not by the conversant on the phone.

What was I thinking, expecting a flood of calls to a radio audience of thousands of people? I should have known better!

"BASHFUL BLADDER"

Nurses and others who work in medical offices have long been aware that some individuals are unable to produce urine samples. This phenomenon, sometimes called "bashful bladder," paruresis, is the inability to urinate in public restrooms. It is most common in males; various studies suggest a range of frequency from 14 to 32 percent of males.[4] Within this spectrum, some simply experience delayed urination and must wait for their need to void to overcome their anxiety, while others are unable to urinate at all. The effects of external variables are highly individual as well—some people are only stricken when other people are within a certain range of proximity, some can urinate in the presence of strangers but not friends or family, some the other way around, some are completely at ease in a stall where there is visual but not auditory privacy, for some the lack of auditory privacy is the great inhibitor, and some are simply unable to use public restrooms, period, whether or not others are in the room.

"Bashful bladder" syndrome is well known to our anxiety patients. Not only are many of them unable to use the restroom in public or semipublic places or in other people's homes, but a surprisingly high number are similarly inhibited in their own homes as long as someone might be able to hear them. The physiological expression of the anxiety is a complete failure of function—and while this can be a minor nuisance in some settings, for some people it is a problem of such magnitude that it requires major alterations in lifestyle. For example, one man and his wife agreed that his wife would move to the other side of the house, away from the bathroom, so he could void successfully.

Helene, who had been a widow for many years, found herself profoundly lonely and resolved to break through her inhibitions and make a second bid for happiness, but she could not overcome the obstacle of "bashful bladder." She met a very patient, very kind man, John, who was shy himself and charmed by her reticence. They proceeded very cautiously—as you might imagine—and Helene was pleased to report that she had spent several "lovely evenings" with her suitor. Her hopes were smashed, though, when she made dinner for him at her house and experienced an evening of increasing physical discomfort. She was unable to use the bathroom with John in the house even if they were on separate floors. Though she managed to get through a long after-dinner conversation filled with wine and romantic suspense, finally and quite abruptly, with no explanation, Helene asked John to leave. That was the end of the romance.

For many afflicted by anxiety about urination, work and school situations are unnerving or intolerable. Dormitory life becomes a nightmare, and attendance at sports events, concerts, theater, and other public get-togethers involve agonies of discomfort, both psychological and physical. One only has to conjure up the typical scene in the restrooms at sporting events— especially in men's rooms, where individuals line up four or five people deep to use ten urinals.

Most of my patients with these fears use stalls where they are not visible; and some may need to wait for long periods before managing to urinate. Over the years, I have been amazed at the complex calculations some people have devised to regulate fluid intake and timing to restrict the need to urinate. They describe themselves as *never* comfortable and *always* distracted by either the need or the fear of the need to urinate. Further, they spend a great deal of time learning the locations of the most isolated and unused restrooms at work, school, and recreational facilities, and research the times when these are least likely to be in use. Likewise, students in dormitories or fraternity houses have told me that they routinely wake in the middle of the night or at dawn or miss meals in order to have the bathrooms to themselves.

"Bashful bladder" is not well understood and sufferers find it hard to explain the problem, knowing only that normal function eludes them. The physiology of urination is complex, requiring simultaneous action of the sympathetic and parasympathetic components of the autonomic nervous system to relax the urethra and contract the muscles of the bladder. It is possible, of course, for any anxiety to disrupt this normal function, but urination is seldom inhibited in other types of fearful situations.

Some studies correlate this problem with "body shyness," in which individuals experience discomfort undressing, showering, and the like in the presence of people of the same sex. However, some of my patients argue convincingly that they are not overly embarrassed by routine body functions. Instead, their self-consciousness and over-alert monitoring of the usually automatic function of urinating may "confuse" the flow of neuronal messages to the bladder. An analogy, for most people, would be the disruption in swallowing that occurs when they focus on the mechanisms of swallowing. Another situation, which has its own great significance in the lives of many socially phobic people, is impotence, discussed later in chapter 5.

In speculating on the meaning of the "bashful bladder" syndrome, writers have posed a variety of psychoanalytic explanations, including an inability to express hostility, an unconscious equation of urination with sexuality, and "an internalized desire for punishment." A more compelling explanation may lie in a possible link to the territorial struggle of animals. Many animals urinate on areas of their territory to communicate information to others about boundaries. Is it possible that urinating in the presence of others of our own species evokes inborn competitive fears? Urination may be perceived as an unconscious challenge that the socially fearful individual dares not issue. Fascinating as such a possibility is, we still know too little about our species and the myriad signals we communicate to each other daily to explain the meaning of "bashful bladder."

EATING IN PUBLIC

An elderly patient came into our clinic desperate for help. She feared she would have to give up her bridge club, an important activity in her life. Several years ago, she discovered that she could no longer pour coffee without shaking, but she managed to place it on the table so her guests could help themselves. Whether or not this tremor stemmed solely from anxiety or was in part a physiological symptom of aging was not clear, but her humiliation and attempts to avoid displaying it were clear indications of social phobia. Even more distressing was her growing fear of choking—she found herself completely unable to eat and had to content herself with sipping coffee. But soon even this became impossible—she began to fear that her cup would rattle in the saucer or that she would spill her coffee or, again, begin to choke, thus displaying her anxiety.

Studies show that an inability to eat in the presence of others is one of the most common fears of social phobics.[5] Most usually complain that they are unable to eat in restaurants, but some find it difficult or impossible to eat at home with invited guests, family members, or, in the most extreme cases, even parents or spouses. Believing they are under constant scrutiny by dinner companions, these individuals agonize over a number of things: that their hands will tremble visibly; that they will spill their food or miss their mouths; that they might choke, vomit, or lose control of their bowels. As one might imagine, the more elegant the setting and the more socially "prominent" the company, the greater is the potential for disaster. Here the possibility of failure in the presence of someone considered to be important takes on a primary concern.

Like people with bashful bladder, social phobics with eating problems describe complex strategies to hide evidence of their disorder. They begin by carefully selecting the restaurant or set- ting for the meal—it must be uncrowded and informal; a booth is preferable. Even what to order is an issue—soups, pastas, or hand-eaten items are universally avoided. One woman told me that, for her, serving with a ladle was an ordeal. As for beverages, something in a hefty container conceals hand tremors. Champagne glasses, wine goblets, and delicate teacups are out!

As with other specific social fears, it is usually difficult or impossible, even in psychotherapy, to track the anxiety about eating in public back to its source. But in the case of one patient, there was no question. At the age of twelve, she received permission from her parents to invite a friend over for dinner. During the course of the meal, she accidentally spilled food on the floor. Enraged, her father forced her to place her plate on the floor and finish the meal there, saying, "If you're going to act like a dog, then eat like a dog." From that day forward, she was never able to eat in front of nonfamily members again. Whenever she tried, she choked violently and sometimes even vomited. The fear of such episodes grew so intense that she became a near recluse. Of course, few people can point to such specific casual events. In this woman's case, the father's tantrum may have activated or reinforced a latent tendency in her neuro- physiologic makeup.

Not until one eschews all invitations and other opportunities to share meals with others does it become apparent how much of human social life is bound up with the sharing of food. Many group-living animals have highly developed rituals around food: how it is eaten, by whom and who eats in what order. Can these behaviors be precursors of *our* manners and conventions?

COVERING UP SHYNESS

I can usually identify socially phobic people at our first meeting, but some patients are less easily identified. Their voices are strong, their handshakes firm, and their initial gazes direct. As we talk, however, their behaviors change. They seem to shrink back and begin avoiding eye contact. They often explain that while they may appear to others to be extroverts, their surface appearance is "not really" them. Their outward behavior is a complete act, they tell me. Inwardly, they are anxious and frightened that the secret of their true, timid selves will be discovered. Like the terrified actor who accomplishes a flawless performance, the person who compensates on the outside for extreme distress within falls into a special category that I call *compensated* social phobia.

In his book *Conquering Shyness*, the psychologist Jonathan Cheek quoted film actress Valerie Kaprinsky's explanation of compensation: "When I was going to acting school, I was so shy I couldn't do anything without feeling ridiculous. I broke out of it when I understood once I was on stage in front of the camera I could do anything, because it wasn't me. I had an alibi for the part."[6]

This kind of reliance on "acting" to compensate for the otherwise debilitating aspects of social phobia is common among the clients at the anxiety clinic. However, the degree to which and the circumstances in which such acting "works" vary considerably. David, described in an earlier chapter, got by in his medical practice by "acting like a doctor." A hotel receptionist, Amy, told me that as long as she "acted like a receptionist should," she could interact with hotel guests. But perhaps the most dramatic example of compensation for social phobia was a patient who had earned her way through college by dancing in a topless bar. When I expressed surprise, she explained that she knew she was a good dancer. "I love being a dancer—I mean, I love playing the role. It's what I always wanted to be, and when I'm up there, I know I'm doing what I do best." In focusing on the dancing itself, she was able to exclude thoughts about evaluative scrutiny, but in the privacy of her own home, with a boyfriend with whom she felt safe and trusted in every other way, she was unable to have sex with the light on.

Other people with social phobia report that they are able to "say the right thing" and even "play the life of the party." This sort of role playing *can* work and may allow one to be functional, but—like the professional actor who suffers invisibly from stage fright—inside, the person is still experiencing near-crippling anxiety.

Such compensation is imperfect for another reason as well: it may work in certain situations only. For example, Amy, the hotel receptionist, was able to appear comfortable behind the counter, but she was unable to move up to a management position because she was unable to conceive of how a manager was supposed to "act."

Taking up a role appears to structure stressful situations for the anxious person. Role playing provides the appropriate lines to speak, but also permits a sense that "it's not really me," a sense that removes some of the responsibility for the situation. Acting also seems to divert the person's attention from the signs and symptoms of arousal and anxiety, permitting a fuller focus on performance. While useful in the short run, however, such role playing could actually *prevent* the sufferer from developing better means of dealing with the problem and finally overcoming the anxiety.

One final disadvantage of this kind of uneasy compensation is that it renders the resultant social interaction a little unreal. The pleasures of social interaction include the gradual growth of intimacy between people, and intimacy in turn is fostered by mutual, and truthful, self-disclosure. If the sum total of a person's contribution to an exchange is actually inauthentic role playing, the possibility that the experience might evolve into a meaningful relationship is greatly restricted. Although it is true that many socially phobic people are less concerned with developing full-blown friendships than with simply getting through a social encounter without humiliating themselves, the potential for *real* socializing to enhance and enrich their lives encourages us to try to resolve debilitating social anxiety on a deeper level.

Chapter 4

Joining the Group at School and Work

He dare not come in company, for here he should be misused, disgraced, overshoot himself in gesture or speeches or be sick; he thinks everyman observes him.
                    —Richard Burton, *The Anatomy of Melancholy*

S OCIAL PHOBIA MOST OFTEN manifests itself in the late teens. There are some logical reasons for this. In the middle-class American model most studied by social researchers, teenagers tend to remain within the security of the family group. Although separating from one's family is part of adolescent development, how far to go from home, or whether to move away at all, is often up to the discretion of each child. Additionally, along with many parents, adolescents tend to lack the education to recognize a treatable problem. And even if they do wish for help in dealing with the outside world, they generally lack the resources to find or secure it on their own.

But aside from practical considerations, there are more fundamental, evolutionary reasons for the fact that social phobia emerges most frequently in late adolescence. Separation is only one aspect of teenagers' developmental task; another task is to find one's place in one's *peer* group—in anthropological terms, among one's own age mates. The main psychological issues during the high school years involve competition with one's peers—and therefore the first serious assessments of one's own strengths and weaknesses as they compare with those of individuals in one's own age group. For one who perceives him- or herself as hopelessly weak, lacking the skills to compete in this first group outside the safety of the family, school can be viewed as a gantlet to be run every day, and classrooms as torture chambers.

THE ORDEAL OF SCHOOL

Shy young children complain of stomach aches, headaches, sore throats, and other anxiety symptoms in their attempts to avoid school (I'll return to these in a later chapter). The teenagers we see at our anxiety clinic describe long delays in the shower, over-long periods of anxious self-scrutiny in the mirror, and complex postponement maneuvers every morning—all vain efforts to put off leaving home. For them, even solitude in an unhappy family is preferable to the draining presence of age mates, which brings the continual anxiety-provoking self-evaluation, peer assessment, and comparisons that are unavoidable in the group experience. Typically, Mondays witness the onset of these symptoms, whereas weekends and holidays offer respites from them.

Arrival at school calls for exquisite timing. Getting there too early invites casual social contact; arriving late means walking into a crowded classroom and drawing all eyes at once. Socially fearful teens describe themselves as caught up in an exhausting decision-making process from the moment they wake up. "How long shall I take to shower, eat breakfast, walk to school?"

But these solitary morning rituals of anxious anticipation and planning pale next to the thought of being called on in class. One girl explained, "Usually I knew the material forward and backwards. I could have answered any question standing on my head. If I wasn't so terrified, I suppose I could have even been a show-off. But if she called on me I might as well have been a baboon—the answers would fly out of my head and I would be a stuttering idiot. Sitting there with everybody watching me, the most I could ever say was, 'I don't know.'"

In the effort to avoid the teacher's notice, selecting classes (where there is a choice) and deciding where to sit in the classroom are crucial. These students "research" their electives, not to determine their relevance to their personal academic interests or goals or the quality of the teaching, but rather to determine whether oral presentations are required. Are students called upon in class? Does the teacher tend to call on people who do not speak up? Does the teacher pressure, criticize, or embarrass students? Is the class large enough for a quiet student to avoid notice?

In these ways, a lifelong pattern is established, to avoid notice and especially scrutiny (real or imagined). In the process, personal attributes, talents, interests, and the exposure to life experiences that yield unexpected pleasures and directions all receive short shrift, and the foundations of the invisible walls that circumscribe the socially phobic individual's narrow life are laid down.

Many socially phobic people choose educational paths and eventually careers solely in terms of their social anxiety. One researcher studying shy students determined that his subjects took a distinctly passive approach to their own educational development and failed to use available resources such as academic advisers or counselors because of their fear of authorities. Their avoidance led, ultimately, to a sense of discouragement.[1] If they managed to enter higher education, their course and career selections were dramatically tilted toward fields perceived as involving the least social interaction, for example, computer-related work, accounting, bookkeeping, word processing, and various types of research.

This tense dance of avoidance and self-protection causes many socially phobic people to drop out of school early. Some of my patients obtained their GED (graduate equivalency degree) certificates with home study after dropping out; others have a history of long, painful disputes with their families over "throwing themselves away." One study showed that 83 percent of socially phobic subjects were restricted by their anxieties in school activities and academic functioning.[2] Failure in the school system reinforced their movement away from the group. Along with parents, most teachers and school administrators are unaware of social phobia as a discrete condition, and so the assessments they record for these students have ranged from "malingering" to "schizophrenic," labels that reflect the extreme avoidance, awkwardness, and *seeming* desire for isolation that these anxious students exhibit.

Oral Presentations

In most socially phobic people, both the anxiety around people and attempts to avoid social contact build over time, but many point to a single moment or event that marks for them the "beginning" of the disorder, a "last straw" that causes them to give up the internal struggle with their fears. Most commonly, among my patients, this psychological Waterloo occurs in high school, usually in a speech or drama class when a student has been unable to find a way around giving an assigned speech, recitation, or performance.

One bright nineteen-year-old man described his high school years. "I have had severe nervousness around people as long as I can remember. Grade school and high school were absolute torture for me, although I did my homework, studied hard, and knew that I was smart. I would spend all my time living in mortal fear of being called on or somehow singled out by teachers. To be the center of attention in those moments was my worst possible nightmare."

A young woman told me, "Early in my senior year we were assigned oral book reports. I chose *To Kill a Mockingbird*, my favorite book. I'd read it three times and loved it. I knew why I loved it. I knew why others would love it. But all that was beside the point. It started when the teacher assigned the date for my presentation. I spent three weeks dreading it. I couldn't think of anything else, I couldn't sleep, I wrote out my speech on index cards over and over again. I knew I was going to make a fool of myself—I could *see* myself doing it. And when the day came, I could hardly make myself speak. The whole time I was giving my report people in the back kept yelling, 'Louder!' I sweated, became short of breath, got dizzy, and my mind froze. I got through the rest of my report in a whisper. Shortly after that I dropped out of school and have been working on a highway crew. This is not where I wanted to be in my life, and my parents are so disappointed in me we don't even talk much anymore. At times I think I must have some sort of illness and that I should have the will power to get over it. I think about suicide all the time."

This description is characteristic. Typically, apprehension mounts unbearably, and at the time of the presentation, when anxiety recedes for most normal people, anxiety fails to wane and may even worsen, leading to stammering, perspiring, blushing, shaking, freezing—or the fear of these things happening. The mind seems to go blank in terror. Most say that they managed to finish the task somehow, although some cut it short or flee, feigning illness.

It is during these dreadful moments that a sympathetic, positive response by a teacher or even a classmate—indicating a positive rather than negative assessment—might turn the tide. But if somebody laughs, comments critically, displays boredom or discomfort, the sufferer's anticipation of negative evaluation is seen as having been justified. As a result, most often, the person never again voluntarily puts him- or herself into the position of being evaluated and compared. In many cases, this last straw causes the person to drop out of school.

The decisions made by socially anxious adolescents appear to set the pattern for the rest of their lives. In a fascinating study of the "life-course patterns" of shy children, the developmental psychologist Avshalom Caspi and colleagues followed individuals over thirty years who had been identified as shy and reserved in late childhood. They expected shy children to encounter difficulties during late adolescence and young adulthood, the period in which it is normal to assume the adult roles associated with marriage, parenthood, and career. Would childhood shyness have an effect on how an individual made the transition to adulthood?

The researchers looked at men and women separately. They found that the men in their study who had been reluctant to enter social settings as children appeared, in general, to be reluctant to enter the new and unfamiliar social settings required to become husbands, parents, or members of the work world. The majority of the shy women were likely either to have no work history at all or to have stopped working permanently when they married or had a child. The researchers concluded that childhood shyness prompts women to select a more domestic lifestyle than their peers and to avoid seeking work outside the home.[3]

As I will explore in chapter 5, for women, the symptoms of social anxiety seem remarkably compatible with the classic submissive role of stay-at-home wives and mothers that are now fading from our society, whereas for men these symptoms come into lifelong conflict with the demands of the masculine role. It is my guess that, with nonworking mothers already the exception rather than the rule, these gender differences in the life-course patterns of the socially anxious will gradually disappear.

LEAVING SCHOOL

Although leaving school might bring some immediate relief to the socially phobic, in the long run the difficulties increase. Once one moves out into the world of work or college, one begins to confront more hierarchies with both formal and informal delineations in rank. Examples of ranks are easy to find in college settings, where competition for resources is not simply subliminal but explicit. Consider the increasingly intense battle for entry into college and professional schools. Once in, students are confronted with ranking systems that indicate precisely where one stands—medical training, for instance, breaks down into premedical students, medical students, residents, nurses, doctors, senior staff, and so on, all with a clear and acknowledged status. In universities, the hierarchy consists of students, teaching assistants, instructors, assistant professors, associate professors, full professors, department heads, deans, and so on. In business and industry there are entrance positions, middle-management positions, executives; vice-presidents, board members, and so on. The military is perhaps the prototype of the ranking system inherent in our human groups, and many workplaces and civilian enterprises are modeled on it (police departments, for example).

These formalized measures of status stimulate self-evaluation and the assessment of others in everybody—evolutionarily speaking, that is what they are for. Carl Sagan and Ann Druyan describe these remnants of social hierarchy in humans as the "frozen memory of past coercions."[4] For socially anxious people, once out of school and in the "real" world, the opportunities for negative self-assessment increase dramatically. Job interviews, for example, are specifically designed to afford potential employers the opportunity to assess and evaluate applicants.

UNDER SCRUTINY AT WORK

Getting up in the morning and heading out the door into the wider world is a survival strategy that most of us share. And yet for the socially phobic, stepping outside is a daily struggle and putting in the requisite eight hours at work is agony. Fearful or not, however, somehow or other, they rise every morning—often after spending an anxiety-wracked night—to perform whatever rituals they have devised to propel themselves into joining the workforce. Although the need to earn a living is a powerful motivator, the personal costs to "keep on keeping on" do not diminish for these people over time. One young woman related that she vomited every weekday morning and struggled with herself each workday about calling in sick.

But despite the intensity of the private struggle, the fact that working for a livelihood is so closely associated with survival means that people who suffer social phobia on the job do not give in easily to their fears. In one study, patients averaged *seventeen years* of symptoms before seeking treatment—seventeen years of anxious insomnia, forcing themselves every morning to ignore the biological force of clamoring autonomic responses, feelings of dread, and catastrophic thoughts that are the body's alarm system.[5]

When they finally do ask for help, it is commonly a change of job, setting, responsibilities, or supervision that precipitates a visit to our clinic. Many of our clinic patients are already on disability leave when they come in, having given up work on their own or because they have been threatened with termination. In 1986, researchers at another anxiety clinic reported that 92 percent of their socially phobic patients suffered some other occupational disability in addition to their anxiety.[6] People who are phobic in work situations do not find it easy to seek help. Often they have managed with great discomfort and imaginative maneuvering to tolerate the feared situations or avoid their most terrifying aspects. They may have refused transfers, promotions, or higher paying job offers in order not to disturb the delicate adjustment that has enabled them to keep from bolting and running.

Socially anxious people work in all sorts of occupations: they include laborers, factory workers, teachers, executives, and many others. Professional workers tend to seek help most often, probably because they are most likely to be involved in situations where they must meet new people and give presentations. Those who seek help for social phobia at work are most likely to be men, even though evidence suggests that a slightly larger proportion of females make up the population of socially phobic people as a whole.

As the gender patterns in the workforce continue to shift, and women begin to share more equitably the society's leadership roles, we can expect this imbalance to even out. Several studies suggest a negative relationship between leadership and shyness or social anxiety. The psychologist Philip Zimbardo studied cadets at a U.S. military academy; those who rated themselves as shy scored lower than others in leadership effectiveness. Also, preschool teachers who rated their four-year-old students noted that shy children exhibited less leadership ability than nonshy peers.[7] Though these findings might seem self-evident, they have special significance in the work setting, suggesting that social anxiety may have subtle effects on qualities particularly desired in the workplace. Authority is a major elicitor of social anxiety, and nowhere in our lives do we meet authority as much as in our respective workplaces. Socially phobic women may find ways to "hide out" and camouflage their anxieties in the traditional role as at-home wife and mother, but once out in the workforce their disorder can be expected to impede them from advancement in ways similar to their male counterparts.

PERFORMING BEFORE OTHERS

Not all performances occur in the entertainment world. As I pointed out in the last chapter, the world increasingly expects and demands that ordinary people take the podium and conduct themselves as public figures. In the work arena, jobs often depend on the ability to stand up in public and account for oneself, even though by training and inclination the person may have prepared for a worklife of quiet, even solitary concentration. Like the students described earlier, adult patients describe their tortured anticipation of upcoming speeches, their exaggerated, often compulsively repetitive rehearsals, and their typical "overorganization" even for very brief presentations. As a result of this anxious preparation, many of the dreaded events go well, but when patients look back they recall a string of "close calls" and near failures. Again, there is usually a "final straw," brought about by a job change or a change in process that suddenly makes public interactions more necessary. Many socially phobic performers are finally overwhelmed and seek help. However, those less informed, or less courageous, may simply withdraw, quit, or remain stuck for many years without advancing.

John, a thirty-five-year-old married business school graduate, had worked for seven years as a stock analyst in a large investment firm. His work consisted of reviewing corporate reports, "crunching numbers" at the computer, and writing recommendations for buying or selling stocks and bonds. But the year before he came to our clinic, John had joined a small group of financial analysts who had started their own company with high hopes of really hitting it big. Because of John's experience and expertise, the group looked to him as the logical person to present their ideas and plans to groups of potential investors.

John had spent the majority of his working life alone hunched over sheaves of paper or staring intently at a computer screen. He had certainly never thought of himself as outgoing, but he did not consider his "quietness" and preference for solitude to be a problem until this new responsibility fell to him. He had never before had to stand up in front of a group and hold forth. For the first few presentations he prepared and rehearsed to the point where "I could recite the material in my sleep," and at the meetings he did well with a minimum of discomfort.

But soon each presentation began to loom, and gradually the very thought of one triggered anxiety symptoms. John would perspire, feel weak, and hear a tremor in his voice. "In the beginning," he told me, "I could ignore what was happening inside me and just get through. Things went okay in the presentations—or in most of them. There were good days and bad days, although I couldn't tell you what made them different. Sometimes I'd have no problems—I'd feel strong and confident and know I was coming across that way, but other times even before I started I knew it was going to be a torture chamber. I just had to grit my teeth and get through it."

The lack of predictability that John experienced occurs in some patients and not in others. Some say, "When I wake up in the morning, I don't know whether I'm going to have a good or bad day or whether I'll be able to handle the thing I fear or not." As yet, no satisfactory explanation accounts for this fluctuation in anxiety levels, but observations suggest that unpredictability adds yet another concern to the preoccupied self-monitoring: "Am I going to survive the presentation or not?"

Gradually, John's bad days overtook his good ones. When I asked what he meant by "bad," he described the usual physical symptoms, plus an addled, disorganized quality to his thinking— or a "block" altogether. He became unnerved when he realized that "sometimes I had no idea what I had just said." This terrifying sense seems to combine "what if" catastrophic thinking about the present with a loss of focus on the present. Some people report "no thought," a closing down of the ability to sustain an ongoing line of reasoning.

For a while, although John's colleagues had no idea that he was suffering ("As long as it doesn't show I still have a shred of dignity left"), John was able to shift attention to one of his partners when he became too agitated to continue. However, a few months before he entered treatment, the partners had decided that John ought to be presenting on his own—there was no need for anyone else to accompany him. "At that point my safety net was gone," he said. "That's when I started drinking myself to sleep."

Just before I met John, he had called in sick on the day of a presentation for the third time. At that point he realized that his fears were threatening to wreck not only his but his partners' future. Realizing that he was unable to control his reactions despite the high stakes was the insight that enabled John to admit to a need for professional help.

At our clinic, John began using a medication used for social anxiety called generally clonazepam (discussed in detail in chapter 10) and participated in a social anxiety treatment group. Within several months he had returned to giving his usual presentations at work. He decided to stop drinking and said that he was enjoying life much more fully than before. He looked back on the days before treatment as unbearably constricted by his social fears. John's recovery was complete, and it delighted him at a family gathering to hear his relatives confirm his feeling that he seemed to be indeed "a new man."

STATUS: IN THE BEHOLDER'S EYE

A few social phobics fear people, period. More, however, are finely attuned to gradations in status and the fear grows more intense as the perceived status of the audience goes up. In this context, "status" is in the eye of the beholder. For some, it is age and wisdom. For others, it is wealth, expertise, educational levels, or certain levels of professional or purely financial success.

Ned was a fifty-six-year-old dentist who had been in practice for twenty-nine years. The story he told was of a career completely wrecked by his growing fear of "doing something foolish." He felt that this could occur at any time, but he was particularly worried about how he conducted himself at work in front of patients whom he considered as holding greater status—as reflected in the type of insurance they carried—than himself. He could work with relative ease on welfare patients, but not those who paid privately or carried private insurance. He denied being prejudiced against or biased toward those on welfare; rather he explained that he was simply "aware" of their status and that that was enough. (Another man who came to our clinic exemplified how subtly status is registered in the eye of the beholder: he had difficulty talking with tall, gray-haired men, considering them "dignified" and therefore threatening.) Specifically, Ned feared that in treating his high-status dental patients his hands would shake, he would perspire, and, to his extreme embarrassment, his anxiety would be obvious to his successful patients, who, he believed, were "completely at home in the world" and had never endured an anxious moment in their lives.

Although he tried to control his fear by keeping himself ignorant of his daily schedule of patients, he almost always failed in his attempts to stay away from the appointment book. If he saw on the next day's list the name of one of his "successful" patients, he felt a stab of fear that he knew would turn into a bout of horrible insomnia that night. When the person was one of high status *and* the procedure was a particularly complicated one, the formula for terror was complete. Ned lay awake imagining himself being humiliated by his own trembling hands. The next day, exhausted and emotionally drained, he would complete the procedure in a cold sweat.

He was unable to say for sure whether anyone ever noticed his discomfort, but he felt "they really must have." Over the years he had developed a variety of strategies: even though his staff complained regularly, he kept the air conditioner at high levels to minimize his sweating, and he had hired other young dentists to perform the more difficult procedures, with himself acting as "consultant."

Although more comfortable at home and on weekends, Ned lived in dread that a patient might call with a dental emergency or, worse yet, a complaint about his work. Eventually, Ned sold his practice in the hopes of gaining some relief from his constant anxiety. But he was simply unable to find another pursuit that did not involve social interaction and the possibility, as he saw it, of humiliation. Nor could he easily follow his dream to travel after retirement—fearful that his hand would shake, he was unable to register at hotels or use his credit card.

But perhaps the cruelest subtheme of Ned's struggle was his wife's complete disgust with the whole situation. Far from empathizing, she demanded that he toughen up and "act like a man." When he gave up his practice, she threatened to leave him—but stayed and made his life even more miserable by ridiculing his weaknesses and fears. This problem occurs for many socially phobic patients. Not only do they feel unable to explain or control their fears; their families and loved ones often interpret their experiences as nothing more than silly self-indulgence.

Ned's wife's reaction highlights a common problem for social phobics. Most find it nearly impossible to convey the intensity of their fears to others who do not share their high levels of social anxiety. On the face of it, Ned was an experienced, competent, mature practitioner who most would consider far beyond concerns about others' evaluations. To his wife, his explanations sounded "ridiculous"—flimsy, unlikely, childish, and incomprehensible. Faced with trying to convey their anxieties to their loved ones, many socially fearful people make excuses or claim to have different kinds of problems. Families who fail to support or help, especially when they actively express disapproval or disbelief, add shame, impaired self-esteem, and depression to the patient's difficult experience. In the extreme, the lack of empathy may lead to drug and alcohol abuse, divorce, deep despair, and suicidal thoughts.

Ironically, for Mary, a high school chemistry teacher, the people who set her terror in motion were those who occupied her own status niche. Mary had been named Teacher of the Year in her large urban high school. A popular teacher with a casual, comfortable style among students, she was perfectly at ease with her students, and laughed and joked with them easily. Teaching unobserved by others in her peer group had given her her happiest and most fulfilling moments, but she figured she had missed approximately two years of school out of the preceding ten because of her high anxiety surrounding observers. If the principal, another teacher, a parent, or any other adult entered her room, Mary became completely unable to function.

Open house evenings and parent/teacher conferences were unnerving ordeals, and Mary had pleaded sick consistently over the past two years to avoid them. Her principal had assigned her to run the annual science fair and to be present on the evenings when the parents visited. This was sheer hell, and the third year Mary, offering no explanation, refused to take on the job. Humiliated by her own anxiety, defeated by the undiminishing anxiety she felt about being scrutinized and—as she perceived it—continually evaluated, she had chosen to appear stubborn and recalcitrant rather than risking the possibility that her principal might discern the truth. Again, by the time Mary sought treatment, her life's work as a teacher—"it's all I can do, I'm one of those 'born teachers'"—was at serious risk.

For some people with social phobia, merely being seen triggers anxiety. But others need only *believe* that they are being observed or that there is a *possibility* that they might be seen to feel fear; many believe that they are under observation much of the time. They frequently admit that such a perception "sounds paranoid," but nevertheless are convinced that others notice them, watch them, and criticize them to an abnormal degree. This ability to question the reality of their belief, by the way, distinguishes them from truly paranoid patients.

Al, a thirty-year-old single man, came into the clinic saying he needed help for his problems at work. He had served for seven years as a machinist in a tool and die company. For about the first six months of that time he had worked days, and despite the fact that his boss raved about his craftsmanship, Al was in constant fear that a foreman or co-worker could step up at any time and watch him work. Just a glance his way would cause Al to sweat, shake, and become clumsy, terrified that "I'm going to screw up." Thinking about and anticipating these encounters put him constantly on the brink of calling in sick, but instead he took to drinking or smoking marijuana in the mornings before work to "calm his nerves."

Al really liked and trusted his boss, and finally he managed to tell him a bit about his problem without completely mortifying himself. The foreman was sympathetic and moved Al to a machine that was shielded from the view of the twenty other machinists in the shop. Although this did reduce the possibility of "being seen," it actually added to the problem by making Al "feel like a fool" all the time. "Why would a grown man need to hide all day in order to do his work?" he asked himself. He had no answer for his question and felt that he was going crazy. Finally, he talked to his boss again, who suggested that he work by himself in the plant at night. This in itself was a measure of how much the foreman valued Al's work.

The move to the night shift solved Al's work problem—he could work quickly and expertly all night long alone in the shop. But after seven years, he realized he was, as he put it, "holing up from life." Working all night and sleeping most of the day kept him from doing everything but eating solitary meals in front of the television set. Though he saw himself as getting married some day, he had no opportunities to meet single women. "I'm becoming a kind of night creature," he said. "I'm up when the rest of the world is sleeping. It's kind of eerie—and I'm afraid if I don't go back soon I'll *never* go back."

Al was right. He was using the night shift to avoid social contact. His story draws attention to the fact that socially phobic people suffer from their self-imposed isolation. They are not hermits who care nothing about interactions and prefer a solitary existence. Rather, they describe heartbreaking lives of loneliness, and loneliness is often their first complaint upon seeking help.

Following a limited course of treatment, Al returned to the day shift and cautiously began dating. A year and a half later, he called to tell me had a steady girlfriend: "I'm in the land of the living again." Sometime later, Al brought his girlfriend in to a session with me, announcing that they were to be married. She thanked me for being part of his treatment. "For a long time I wanted Al to ask me out but I really believed he didn't like me. When he told me later that he couldn't talk when I was around, I didn't believe it. But I'm beginning to understand what he has been living through, and I'm so glad he lives in the daytime now."

COPING STRATEGIES

Other kinds of social fears besides performance anxiety cause difficulty in the work setting. For some socially phobic patients,

meeting new people and interacting with bosses are most difficult. Given their choice, of course, socially anxious people mold
their environments to minimize the encounters they fear, keeping a low profile so as to go unnoticed.

When these coping strategies fail or when the situation
demands other behaviors, some people cope by *mentally* altering
the situation—simply taking themselves out of the picture by
imagining themselves elsewhere. Others say that they assume the
role of a person performing their job—"acting" the part of
receptionist or doctor, for example. If they can go through the
motions of performing their job, they can be more certain of
controlling and concealing their anxiety. So, in an ironic twist,
certain socially phobic people actually *choose* performance over
the risk of revealing their inner turmoil. Playing a part affords
them a measure of control over themselves and a distraction
from the discomfort of the physiological bells and whistles that
make up the human fear response. Indeed, I have met several
socially phobic individuals who, in their leisure time, are
involved in amateur theater.

RECOGNIZING SOCIAL PHOBIA

There's more to work than a job description. Many ancillary
activities occur throughout a workday apart from duties at one's
desk or workstation. The extreme discomfort many sufferers
experience when eating and drinking in the presence of others,
described earlier, can have serious negative effects on overall job
evaluations. People who find these normal social activities too
harrowing to even consider often fail to attend work-related
company picnics or holiday parties, where personal bonds are
forged that reinforce the formal hierarchy. They also turn their
backs on opportunities to eat with fellow employees, distancing
themselves from peer groups at work.

Most often, this reticence is viewed by others as snobbery—
rarely as shyness or fear. So in a disturbing way, the very fears

of negative evaluation that so dominate and shape the socially phobic's behavior actually contribute to elicit that evaluation from others, setting up an insidious cycle. Unfortunately, like Ned's exasperated wife, most people are completely unaware of the existence of social phobia or are baffled by its intensity. As noted in the preceding chapter, spouses or other loved ones hope that the sufferer will "shake it off and get on with life." When the disorder is played out in the workplace, it results in a tremendous was ˙ of human potential and limited productivity. As I often explain to groups of employers, personnel directors, and managers, understanding and learning to recognize social phobia can enable them to "salvage" underachieving employees who might otherwise be valuable to the firm.

The very nature of social phobia—the paralyzing fear of making a fool of oneself—makes the condition hard to recognize. Sufferers are likely to be seen as conceited, standoffish, "not team players," antisocial, or uncommitted. Most social phobics would be amazed to learn they are conveying these impressions, so focused are they on their terror of negative evaluation. But with an awareness of the disorder and its manifestations, schoolteachers, educators, and administrators, and managers in the workplace can begin to ferret out this "hidden" disability, perhaps even finding ways to urge sufferers to get help. With this hope in mind, I end this chapter with a checklist of clues to the presence of social phobia.

- Socially phobic people may appear shy, introverted, relatively nonsocial
- Social phobics normally avoid eye contact and speak little when spoken to
- They avoid being the center of attention, seldom speak in group settings, and may turn down promotions and other acknowledgments with hollow-sounding explanations or no explanation at all
- They may call in sick with notable frequency or have unexplained absences

- They may appear to be particularly anxious when speaking with supervisors or bosses
- Although not all socially phobic people use drugs or alcohol, many do. Sometimes the first sign of the condition is the use of intoxicants at work.

Chapter 5

Social and Sexual Intimacy

'Twere blush, blush, blush with me every minute of the time, when she was speaking to me.

—Thomas Hardy, *Far from the Madding Crowd*

IT WILL COME AS NO SURPRISE to learn that the social/sexual arena is particularly hellish for social phobics; indeed, one that a great many socially anxious people go to great lengths to avoid. And even when they can make themselves physically enter the social arena and attempt to make contact, they are often unable to participate in the complex, highly detailed, and nearly unconscious social rituals that function to lower most people's natural defenses and gradually foster mutual trust. As a result, research demonstrates that shy and socially phobic people have measurably smaller networks of acquaintances and fewer friends than normal. They date less often, have fewer intimate friends of the opposite sex, and are less likely to be married or to have satisfying mating relationships.[1]

But in attempting to account for the troubles that socially phobic people face in becoming close to others, it is important to realize that no evidence suggests that these people are deficient in their ability to become intimate. Rather, almost always their problems lie in negotiating the outer barriers to intimacy—meeting strangers and interacting with them in ways that lead naturally to closeness. Their hyperawareness of being evaluated and their constant, anxious search for signs of criticism inhibit this process greatly, but in situations where, whatever the reason, they do manage to achieve a level of closeness with another person, they can usually enjoy intimacy as well as anyone else.

Therefore, most socially phobic people function well within their families—so much so that, as one patient put it, "My wife just doesn't understand it. She says I turn into someone else, someone she doesn't know, when we're at a party or a social situation." It is only when they face the prospect of being "looked over" by someone outside the circle of safety that their debilitating fears of evaluation and crippling self-criticism begin to kick in.

The result of such diminished social contact is, in a word, loneliness. A national survey in 1982 found that 19 percent of American men and 30 percent of women reported loneliness. A more recent study reveals that 10 percent of the U.S. population suffers from severe and persistent loneliness.[2] The realities—the actual amount of emotional distress and outright suffering—implied by that figure are staggering.

LONELINESS

Loneliness is the yearning distress that occurs when a person's network of social relationships is significantly deficient—in quantity, quality, or both. In its transient form it is a familiar experience, and most people find ways to eradicate it by taking steps to make social contact, according to the sociologist Robert Weiss, who describes loneliness as "distress without redeeming features."[3] If it remains severe and persistent, however, loneliness can be an extremely painful experience that not only undermines psychological well-being but also increases the risk for serious psychological dysfunction.

Loneliness has been linked to a variety of problems—for example, depression, adolescent truancy, behavior problems, unemployment, and suicidal thinking. Studies of loneliness generally find high correlations with low self-esteem, shyness, self-consciousness, introversion, and the lack of assertiveness. These qualities should sound familiar—they correspond to those that typify the socially phobic indi ·dual. But it is not these individual qualities alone but their combined effects that account for the human suffering linked to a psychological disorder. In that view, loneliness—a predictable effect of social phobia—is perhaps the most poignant burden social phobics must bear—and the most pressing reason for drawing attention to social anxiety as a casual factor. To be shut out from the group by an inability to connect is to lose out on those experiences that humans consider the most valuable of all—meaningful, trusting, and deeply pleasurable personal interaction.

SOCIAL BARRIERS

When we look at the specific social challenges that social phobics have difficulty navigating, we see that the "whitewater" lies in communication. For meaningful interaction to occur between people, ideas and emotions have to be embodied in mutually recognizable "signs." Over the course of human evolution, communication signs have developed two modalities. The *verbal* mode is used most often to convey information, while the *nonverbal* mode expresses emotion.

Nonverbal communication, which comprises about 65 percent of all our communications, has been called "a very honest language."[4] As noted by the pioneering psychologist Virginia Satir, this "elaborate and secret code" is "written nowhere, known by none, and understood by all."[5] Other scientists have asserted that nonverbal communication forms the entire basis for human relations.[6] In this unwritten, uncodified language of body movement and facial expression, and often in the verbal mode as well, socially phobic people often lack fluency. They complain, "I don't know the rules everybody else seems to know." With regard to nonverbal "language," their plaint may contain some truth.

Nonverbal behaviors include gestures, movements, stance, facial expressions, physical spacing between speakers, eye contact, and touching, as well as qualities of language such as voice tone, verbal timing, and emphasis. Although most of us are completely unaware of it as we interact in a conversation, we are sending and receiving nonverbal messages.

Greeting and leave-taking rituals are good examples of how nonverbal cues function in social interactions. Investigators Kenden and Ferber, for example, analyzed filmed greetings and found that they contained a series of phases marked by gaze signals and other nonverbal clues. As soon as two acquaintances catch sight of each other, they begin to synchronize their movements. Before moving closer to each other, each offers a head toss, nod, or wave. As they approach, they smile and perhaps shake hands—sending symbolic signals to disarm defense responses to the physical proximity of another.[7]

Looked at even more closely, greeting behavior appears to encompass a pattern that some researchers consider an innate human response.[8] This pattern consists of a gaze toward another person, a smile, lifted eyebrows, and a fast nod of the head—all occurring in about a third of a second. This brief series of actions acts as a "releasor," eliciting the same behaviors from the other person and, as Kenden and Ferber put it, "serving an important function in the management of relationships between people." It is not difficult to see that anyone who has problems with the "management tool" itself will be at a distinct disadvantage in managing interactions with others. And, in fact, many socially phobic patients focus on such rituals as interactions to be avoided at all costs. "I hate being caught at the door," one man told me, "having to go through that big fuss of shaking hands and kissing the women. Whenever I decide not to go somewhere, what decides me is that big fuss at the door."

Like greetings, leave-takings proceed along their own pattern. The communicants break eye contact, shift their bodies, and utter such short sounds as "Oh!" in order to signal their intention to bring the interaction to a close. When the departure moves of one are matched by those of the other, the leave-taking can be accomplished. Verbal "good-byes" are accompanied by head tosses, waves, ar ' mutual gazes.

All the dimensions of nonverbal expression—including body movement, body distance, facial expression, eye behavior, and touching—are coordinated to form a "picture," a totality created and understood by the two participants as a successful conversation. Many of the patients at our anxiety clinic believe that they have difficulty "coordinating" all the components of a communication properly in order to convey their emotions and information accurately. And many socially phobic patients report that they simply do not know how to end a conversation and are unable to accomplish a leave-taking on the nonverbal level for fear of "doing it wrong."

APPROACHING THE OTHER

As these "codes" and "signs" suggest, even casual or purely social interactions are complex and laden with unconscious meaning. When we turn to social interactions involving potential sexual activity, things become even more subtle and complicated—and the opportunities for not only breaking the mood but breaking the unspoken rules increase dramatically.

The opening chapter of the ethologist Helen Fisher's fascinating *Anatomy of Love* is a cornucopia of what she calls the "games people play" in the process of courting. "The essential choreography of human courtship, love, and marriage," she writes, "has myriad designs that seem etched into the human psyche, the product of time, selection, and evolution. They

begin the moment men and women get within courting range—
with the way we flirt." Fisher details the meanings of such universal flirting patterns as "the coy look" on the part of women, "the
chest thrust" on the part of men—matched across the animal
kingdom by the "looming" and "crouching" positions that signal
dominance and approachability, respectively. Above all, Fisher
concentrates on the eyes. She explains that men and women
often stare intently at a potential mate for about two to three
seconds during which their pupils may dilate—a sign of extreme
interest. "The gaze triggers a primitive part of the human brain,
calling forth one of two basic emotions—approach or retreat.
You cannot ignore the eyes of another fixed on you; you must
respond." You may indulge in "displacement behavior," she says,
such as cleaning your nails or tugging at a lock of hair, to dis-
place anxiety while you decide to flee the premises or stay and
play "the courting game."[9]

It takes no detective to imagine how most socially phobic
patients respond to what Fisher calls "the copulatory gaze."[10] Eye
contact is a major problem for social phobics (see chapter 7),
and when they find themselves in courting situations they are
"afraid to look." Their explanations suggest that they fear both
misinterpretation *and* the possibility that the other person will
read their true intent. "If I look too long or too directly at a
woman," one man told me, "then she will think I'm interested in
her sexually." When I asked him whether in those situations that
interpretation might be correct, he acknowledged that it was,
"but I never know whether it is too early for her to know it, or
whether it might be offensive or what."

So it is not the intimacy of the encounter that socially phobic
people fear. Rather, it is the complexity and growing intensity of
the pattern that the gaze and a positive response initiates—the
human mating dance, a "five-part pickup" so named by
researchers who watched countless couples come together and
perform it in a cocktail-lounge setting. When it was completed
successfully, the couples left the bar together, presumably to
engage in sexual intercourse and, potentially at least, perpetuate

the species. This mating ritual begins with a smile—distin-guished by Fisher from other smiles with other meanings by the term "supersmile." The next stage, "recognition," starts when the two gazes meet. Once the eyes lock, the bodies shift to get into talking range. Talk is stage three, but the content is far less important (often completely *un*important) than how it is expressed. For each sex, a high-pitched, melodious voice is the *real* message, signaling sexual interest. Of the verbal stage, Fisher writes, "Talking is dangerous for an important reason. The human voice is like a second signature that reveals not only your intentions but also your background, education, and intangible idiosyncrasies of character than can attract or repel a potential mate in moments."[11]

The socially anxious person fears that something in his or her own voice will somehow make the other flee. One man con-fided, "I would like to have a cool, detached, male-sounding voice, but it never comes out like that. To myself, I sound like a girl, and I'm always afraid that my voice will squeak or that I won't be able to talk at all. How can women want to relate to somebody who can't even talk like a man?" Most people seem to sense the biological importance of the sound of the voice, as Fisher describes it. For one woman, the effort to control her voice, keeping it from ascending into the upper registers, domi-nated her thinking in all encounters with men. "With women at work, I can summon all the authority I need to get the job done, but with men I sound like a little girl—it's a dead giveaway that I'm aware of them sexually."

Stage four is touch, the "mother of the senses." In sharp con-trast to popular understanding, it is usually the woman in a het-erosexual couple who initiates this stage, with a gentle touch to the shoulder, arm, or wrist. Fisher describes this tiny movement eloquently:

> How insignificant this touching looks, yet how important this touching is. Human skin is like a field of grass, each blade a nerve ending so sensitive that the slightest graze can etch into the human brain a memory of the moment. The receiver notices this

message instantly. If he flinches, the pickup is over. If he withdraws, even barely, the sender may never try to touch again. If he ignores the overture, she may touch once more. But if he leans toward her, smiles, or returns the gesture with his own deliberate touch, they have surmounted a major barrier well known in the animal community.[12]

What a tremendous responsibility goes along with this powerful touch, however light! One woman patient told me that she had read in a magazine that touching a man indicated an interest in furthering the relationship. "Just the fingertips on the arm. But I don't know how to do it. I obsess for hours ahead of time about where and when I should touch a man when I go out with him, and when I do touch him, my hands are sweating and I feel so awkward and spastic I'm afraid he'll think I'm slapping him. How do you carry on a conversation with that sort of thing going on in your head? I just don't know how people do it!" The answer is that they lack the exquisite sensitivity of the socially phobic person. For most people the cues that Fisher discusses remain outside conscious awareness.

Once the touch has occurred, "the man and woman begin to move in tandem" and although "this beat of love, of sex, of eternal human reproduction, may be interrupted at any moment . . . if the two are to pass on the thread of human life, they will resume their tempo and continue their mating dance."[13] The objective is total body synchrony—and copulation.

The dance itself is delicate beyond measure, but social phobia reinforces the possibility that the anxiety itself can interrupt the pattern and throw off the building rhythm. The outward impression made by the shy and socially anxious seems cruelly designed to disrupt their courtship efforts. Despite an often desperate wish to make social and sexual contact, the behavioral signals people send are very frequently misinterpreted. The shy— especially males—are seen as less likable and attractive than more outgoing people, and are described as having "many worries and anxieties" or as appearing "thin, weak and frail." Others misinterpret their behavior during social approaches as disinterested, reserved, unfriendly, rejecting, aloof, snobbish, arrogant, or "taken with themselves." Although the people so judged are usually unable to comprehend how their terrified behavior could be so misread, they generally agree that they are unable to convey the right signals—and this concession itself only contributes to the intensity of their anxiety.[14]

CULTURAL BAGGAGE

Both sexes in the United States feel unfairly handicapped by the cultural expectations governing the approach to sexual intimacy. Men tend to feel that women have it easy; women are not expected to make the "first move," and in general, shy girls and women may be seen as demure and even "particularly feminine."[15] Also, they appear lonely, which to some men might signal approachability or even encourage approach.

Males, on the other hand, carry the cultural burden of initiating approach—and frequently socially anxious male patients equate this with the potential for humiliation. "I can't take the rejection," said a successful entrepreneur, presumably inured to the risk of rejection on the business front. "Honestly, I'd rather not try than wind up on the phone trying to carry on a conversation after I've been turned down. I can just picture her on the other end with an expression of disgust or—worse—ridicule on her face." This man had no trouble exchanging pleasantries with businesswomen at work. "I'm a good boss and have very loyal female employees. But when it comes to dating I become emotional. I'd just rather not ask, that's all." On the other hand, women are not always happy with waiting to be approached. "My mother made me go to every high school dance," one young woman told me. "And getting dressed for those functions was like getting dressed for my own funeral. I'd go and stand with the girls and die a thousand times of humiliation. When I graduated and my mother started in on how I should go out for a sorority, I quit college. I wasn't going to set myself up to be shot down any more."

Being rebuffed or rejected may be acutely painful, but not being approached at all or never daring to approach causes cumulative unhappiness leading to despair. One rejection or rebuff may be tolerable, and even—through rationalization— acceptable. But repetitive rejections over time tend to wear away at one's self-esteem, causing chronic unhappiness, constant second guessing about one's own "attractiveness potential," and finally a sense of hopelessness over the possibility of ever developing a love relationship.

Fisher's account of the sex roles played in the so-called five-stage pickup suggests another possible source of discomfort, one that conflicts sharply with traditionally accepted cultural sex-role expectations. She cites the work of Timothy Perper, the biologist who, along with the anthropologist David Givens, studied American men and women in cocktail lounges, regarding the division of labor in the exchange of mating signals:

> American women generally initiate the courting sequence—starting with subtle nonverbal cues such as a slight shift in body weight, a smile, or gaze. Women began two-thirds of all the pickups that Perper witnessed. And the women he later interviewed were quite conscious of having coaxed a potential lover into conversation, touching him carefully here or there, enticing him ever forward with coquettish looks, questions, compliments, and jokes.

Although most people think men are supposed to take the initiative in sexual advances, in practice women around the world actively begin sexual liaisons.[16]

It is possible that the dissonance between this reality and the cultural and social beliefs regarding women's passivity and men's active role may itself contribute to the social phobic's extreme anxiety in the social/sexual world. Socially anxious people exhibit a range of awkward movements—touching the head, face, or body, and nervous shifting of gaze—that interrupts the flow of movements toward easy body synchrony. These difficulties do not reflect a lack of skill or knowledge about dating behaviors, but rather impart a sense of ill ease about the interaction itself. Could it be that those who are extremely socially and sexually anxious are actually more conscious, or at least semiconscious, of both their culturally expected roles (females passive, males active) and their biologically determined roles (females active, males responsive)? Could their heightened awareness of the ambiguity and the opposing signals of cultural and biological impulses be the cause of their unease?

MAKING CONTACT

Once gazes have been exchanged and social contact has been established, a couple begins the talking phase. Socially anxious people initiate fewer conversations, ask fewer questions, and some tend to talk more about themselves than people without anxiety. One person put it this way: "I find myself going on and on, not knowing what I'm saying or where I should stop. I'm hardly aware of what I'm saying until I suddenly realize I've said something completely inappropriate—and then the blushing begins." One young man explained that his last attempts to socialize ended in humiliation when he found himself telling a beautiful woman during the first few minutes of a cocktail-party conversation that he was a virgin.

Others speak *less* than is expected and allow long, uncomfortable silences to elapse, desperately hoping the other will pick up the conversational burden. One woman, a feminist at heart, experienced great shame at adopting the "feminine ploys" of smiling, head nodding, and nervous laughter to get her through tough social situations. She prods herself to be assertive and confident, but "Try as I might to conceal my fears, they seem plainly revealed in my voice—it goes up into the highest register, it sounds like a child's voice, a little girl's voice, and I just can't get control of it." Whatever the perceptions might have been of the men with whom she talked, it was clear that she herself was unable to sustain the gentle, sonorous vocal tones and rhythms that the anthropologist Desmond Morris has called "grooming talk."[17]

For both sexes, if dating opportunities are rare and painfully fraught with anxiety, such situations become emotionally loaded and contribute to a sense of desperation. This feeling combined with the individual's general social isolation tends to translate into extreme dependence and possessiveness once contact has been made.

Henry, a thirty-five-year-old photographer, had known since puberty that he was gay but never had the courage to seek a partner. On location in London for a magazine shoot, Henry encountered Jed, a model. Jed asked Henry out for a drink and confessed a "terrible crush" on Henry. Though there was certainly the potential for a sexual relationship, Jed seemed content to begin with friendship. For years, Henry had been stymied by his inability to approach another man, and although his uninhibited work behind the camera had brought him notable success, he had reached the point at which he was sure he would always be lonely. But now the approach had been accomplished for him by Jed. Perhaps a little out of desperation, Henry immediately fell hopelessly in love. This tendency to rush the situation is common among people with social phobia when they encounter someone who, quite unexpectedly, appears to like them.

Though unable to initiate a sexual relationship, Henry made himself into the world's most attentive friend. Unfortunately, he was so anxious about maintaining the relationship and so nervous about "doing something wrong" that Jed tired of him in a few days. Jed quickly made it known that he felt claustrophobic, smothered, monopolized, and one night he simply got up from dinner at a restaurant and walked out, permanently ending the short-lived relationship. Henry was devastated—and now even less able to contemplate making contact than before.

Henry felt that he had made initial progress by navigating "the approach," but lost his friend by trying too hard. As with many socially phobic people, the slightest confirmation of his greatest fears served to reinforce his generalized social anxiety. When he came to the clinic, he felt sure that he would never again be able to risk humiliation for the sake of friendship or love.

NEGATIVE FEEDBACK

As Fisher's work attests, the social and sexual rituals that underlie our conscious interactive behavior link us with other members of the animal kingdom. Fisher is quite entertaining in her examples: men "puff out," for instance, by leaning back in a chair, locking their hands together behind their heads, and expanding their chests, just as, in their own ways, do many other species.

> Dominant creatures puff up. Codfish bulge their heads and thrust out their pelvic fins. Snakes, frogs, and toads inflate their bodies. Antelope and chameleons turn broadside to emphasize their bulk. Mule deer look askance to show their antlers. Cats bristle. Pigeons swell. Lobsters raise themselves onto the tips of their walking legs and extend their open claws. Gorillas pound their chests. Men just thrust out their chests.[18]

But perhaps each species also has its own particular way of going awry in the mating dance. It is hard to imagine the behavior a flustered lobster or a tongue-tied snake might exhibit, but we do have many examples of what happens to human beings whose courtship impulses are sabotaged from within.

Consider nineteen-year-old Larry, brought into our anxiety clinic by his physician father, who expressed the fear that his son was "schizophrenic." He based his conclusion on what he had observed of his son's social behavior. Larry had recently quit college, returned home, and virtually refused to leave, especially during the daytime. The father described his son as shy since he was a baby. Though he was an outstanding student and athlete, Larry dated only rarely during high school. "Then, when he went away to school, something happened," reported the father. "Some kind of a breakdown—I don't know. I never could get out of him what had happened."

Larry was extremely reticent to discuss his reason for leaving school. Finally, though, I was able to gain his trust and Larry began to recount his history. He had always felt mildly anxious in social situations, he said, and had avoided attention as much as he could. Performing as an athlete was an exception, however, "because it was just doing things I knew I could do well—and I didn't have to speak." But in college he moved into an apartment next door to the house of four young women students. "They were very aggressive, very flirtatious. They decided I was 'cute,' and they just wouldn't let up on me. I used to stay at the library for as long as I could so I wouldn't risk running into one when I came home, but finally my roommate caught on to the fact that I was uncomfortable around the girls, and after that he just wouldn't let up on me either. Finally, mainly to get my roommate off my back, I said I'd go to the movies with him and two of the girls. I was a nervous wreck the whole time, and when we got back home to our place, my date just sat down on the couch next to me and kissed me. I was so nervous already, I don't know why, but I felt my heart race, I started to sweat, and I had to run to the bathroom, where I got sick. All I could think about was that—" Here Larry became very agitated. "I was just totally humiliated by the idea she must have heard me vomiting. I *know* she did. You could hear everything anybody did in that place. That was it. I just couldn't go back. I stayed in the bathroom and I could hear them all talking about how I got sick, that I must be sick. I didn't leave the bathroom until the girls finally went home. I quit school the next day. Now I don't go out at all because I'm afraid there are girls in town who might want to date me. If I see them or they see me, I know I'll get sick again."

Larry described several subsequent instances in which women he considered attractive had greeted him, causing him to become nauseated and tremulous. Avoiding the possibility of getting sick again in the presence of a woman became the governing theme in his life.

The stories of Henry and Larry dramatize the difficulties

socially anxious people have even in the earliest stages of sexual behavior. In this context, it becomes clear why those with social phobia usually have little or no sexual experience and, when they do have a sexual encounter, they receive less satisfaction than nonanxious people.[19] In his studies of shy college students during the 1970s, Zimbardo surveyed shy and nonshy people and found that 60 percent of nonshy students compared to 39 percent of shy students had practiced oral sex and 62 percent of the nonshy versus 37 percent of shy had had sexual intercourse. In one of his surveys, more than one-quarter of the shy women who had had sexual intercourse recalled unpleasant memories associated with it.[20]

Over time, the social anxious come to perceive their sexual experiences as different from those of their peers and then become burdened with doubts as to their sexual desirability and capability. As in Henry's case, the more their negative expectations were borne out, the less able they were to try again. In this way, social anxiety turns sexual encounters into an ever-intensifying vicious circle of distress.

AVOIDANCE AND APPEASEMENT

Sexual encounters may be seen as a microcosm for the whole world of social interaction. For one thing, from the conscious point of view they are unstructured interactions. The unspoken rules for "proper behavior" are uncodified, rarely discussed by parents with children or even, with perfect honesty, among friends. Overall, the success of sexual encounters depends on spontaneous, highly intuitive interaction, whereas for social phobics spontaneity and intuitiveness are almost certain to be extinguished by autonomic nervous system arousal. Thus not only the sending but the interpreting of sexual cues becomes difficult. The situation is only made worse by the unrelenting but completely unrealistic portrayal of sex in the media. "I used to watch pornographic movies," Larry told his therapist, "hoping to learn how to act. But no movies, porno or otherwise, show you how to get from the hallway into the bedroom, from being dressed to undressed, from kissing and caressing to actually having intercourse. My father is a doctor, and he taught me everything there was to know about sex from a physical point of view. But I always felt I was missing the really important information: how to do it without making a complete ass of myself."

If uncertainty and a lack of structure characterize sexual encounters, nudity brings an exquisite vulnerability to them—an inability to hide, both figuratively and literally. In a sexual encounter, both one's real and imagined imperfections are exposed. Needless to say, few of my patients enjoy making love during daylight hours, and some have never allowed a light on at night. One woman told me, "I never wear a bathing suit. I can hardly look at myself in the mirror, even on good days. How can I get naked in front of a man?"

Although social phobia generally renders sexual encounters nearly impossible, for some patients it has the opposite effect. Connie, for example, was in her early twenties when she experienced nearly crippling anxiety in her night classes. She wanted desperately to advance herself professionally and considered the classes imperative, and yet she was failing because she was unable to force herself to participate in the seminars. But as we pursued the source of her problem, aspects of her sexual life were revealed. "It's ironic that I'm so anxious about being around people, men especially, and I get embarrassed so easily, yet I'm what I guess you would call promiscuous."

When asked to elaborate, Connie described her typical Saturday night. She would go out drinking every weekend, depending on the alcohol to subdue her feelings of imminent social disaster. "When I'd get so I could actually get up and dance, inevitably some guy would come up and ask me to and then—well, that's it. They're usually interested in me just because of the way I look, so for the night at least I don't have to worry about saying the wrong thing. In fact, I don't have to worry about saying *anything*. So I go to the guy's place and get it

over with. Then I get up and go home before he can start a conversation about it."

Low self-esteem and a desperate need to be wanted played
their part in shaping Connie's behavior, but the most urgent
motivation for her behavior was her anxious desire to avoid conversation. In her case, mute sex in the dark was preferable to
even the most preliminary verbal exchange with a man. She
could rely on her physical attributes far more soundly than she
could on her ability to carry on a sustained conversation without
revealing her nervousness. And although Connie experienced
no pleasure from the sexual acts themselves, she performed
them as a form of "appeasement behavior," for she dreaded
causing a scene that might draw attention to her by refusing the
man's advances.

This sort of "inadvertent" sexual consent plays a role in some
instances of date rape. The socially anxious have great difficulty
with self-assertion, since their primary motivation is to avoid
making fools of themselves. To raise any sort of a fuss by resist-
ing, yelling, even talking sharply—and thus evoking criticism or
worse, even from the assailant—is simply more difficult than
conceding. This kind of avoidance-appeasement behavior has
also been observed as part of the motivation of shy teenagers,
particularly girls, who seek acceptance through sexuality.

Some evidence indicates that social anxiety has a different
impact on men in the sexual arena. When Zimbardo interviewed
prostitutes about their clients, he found that the women tended
to consider *most* of their customers shy. What criteria did they
use? They described a typical "shy client" as reluctant to initiate
action, awkward about sex, and generally passive. Zimbardo concluded that many men found prostitutes less intimidating than
wives or girlfriends because they were not required to form any
sort of relationship with the prostitutes. In other words, *social*
pressure was absent from the sexual encounter. Furthermore,
the men did not feel the pressure to *perform*—and thus open
themselves to evaluative judgments, as would be the case in the
social/sexual realm.[21] "It's just easier," one man told me. "It may

not be cheaper in the short run but it is in the long run. Because prostitutes don't care what you're like or who you are. All they care about is the money, and that's the way I like it. I might not have any self-confidence with women but I always have plenty of money."

David Barlow, a noted psychologist and leader in the field of anxiety disorders, went a step further by conceptualizing sexual impotence as a form of social phobia—actually a manifestation of performance anxiety. He noted that for a long time researchers and clinicians studying sexual dysfunction had considered anxiety to be a major cause of the failure to achieve an erection. But upon further study, Barlow found the converse: that anxiety itself—not social anxiety specifically, but apprehension and the symptoms of autonomic arousal—actually intensified sexual arousal. Screenwriters and novelists have long exploited this connection by placing their characters in risky trysts, in novel settings, with mysterious, "dangerous" partners.

What interfered, then, with sexual function in impotent men? Further investigation revealed that cognitive interference or distraction—those infuriating, self-critical inner voices commenting on one's own performance—were interrupting these men's sexual function by breaking their concentration.[22] In their pioneering research on sexuality, William Masters and Virginia Johnson called this phenomenon "spectatoring."[23]

Barlow concluded that impotent men appear to be concentrating more on performance-related concerns in their sexual encounters, rather than on erotic cues such as the curve of a breast, the smoothness of skin, the position of limbs, the feel of hair, and particularly "the copulatory gaze." Far from focusing on sexual pleasure, they were condemned to listen to the insistent voices within that asked, "How am I doing?" "What is she thinking?" "Am I doing what she wants me to?" "Is she noticing how fat I am?" "Am I going too fast?" and so on. Rather like test-anxious students who may know the material but are too distracted by their fear of failure to recall the correct answers, impotent men lose their focus on the sexual interchange because of their extreme sensitivity to performance-related cues.

One newly divorced man was overwhelmed by the free-wheeling sexuality open to him after years of faithful marriage. He masturbated frequently, but when he was with a woman, he worried constantly about his ability to have and keep an erection. In his mind, this became the subtheme to every date. He knew how to go through the motions of having a good time and usually felt comfortable enough on his frequent dates to enjoy himself, but throughout the encounter he would be excruciatingly aware of his own state of sexual arousal, wondering whether it was enough to see him through, and the encroaching moment at which it would be put to the test. By the time the dinner and movie were over and the question of sex arose, these concerns would have rendered him sullen and impotent.

"I would suddenly realize that she was expecting me to kiss her. In a split second it would come—the thought that *she* was thinking that I must be gay, since I wasn't responding. Although I've never been remotely interested in homosexual sex, the thought that *she* might think I was made it impossible for me to make a move. And so the whole evening would come to a crashing halt and a humiliating handshake at the door. I can't tell you how many evenings ended in the same way. And of course I was always so embarrassed at the awkwardness, I could never call back. God knows *what* they thought. *They* were probably crushed, come to think of it."

This overriding and inhibiting concern with performance happens to women, too. Many report that their attention during a potential sexual encounter or during sex itself is focused not on the subtle and building sensations of physical and psychological arousal, but rather on the potential for humiliation that they perceive in not being beautiful, sexual, or satisfying enough. So prevalent in our culture is the tendency to view females as the object of male sexuality rather than as equal partners experiencing their own pleasurable crescendo toward orgasm that countless women have internalized this distorted perception. Where social anxiety attunes the woman to the potential for mortification and fills her mind with self-critical thoughts such as "I'm too fat, too old, too ugly," the gradual surrender to pleasure and, ultimately, orgasm is interrupted. Thus, as with the inability to sustain erections in men, two widely reported female sexual dysfunctions—the failure to achieve orgasm and the tendency to "fake it"—are reinforced, if not initiated, by social anxiety. Remembering that social phobia is defined as distress intense enough to cause dysfunction, it is easy to see how certain disorders that have up to now been regarded as exclusively sexual might be understood and treated as expressions of this more generalized condition.

MARRIAGE AND DIVORCE

As the scientific literature strongly confirms, shy and socially phobic people are less likely to marry than people who do not suffer from this disorder. And even when they do marry, they wed later than people who are not shy or anxious about others.[24]

But once the knot is tied, the socially anxious may have very solid and satisfying marriages. One study found that some spouses of the shy viewed typically shy behaviors in a positive light, describing them as "reserved, sensitive, modest, sincere, cautious, dignified, mannerly, or prudent."[25] A marital partner who prefers solitary activities may value his or her socially anxious spouse for that very reason. In fact, I occasionally see partners who have accommodated themselves so completely to their mate's social phobia that successful treatment upsets the balances. One wife told me after her husband's phobia was resolved, "This isn't the man I married, and I'm not so sure I like this version. Some things are better, true. He is more likely to initiate lovemaking, and I like that. But he's also much more talkative and outgoing. He invites people over, wants to go to parties—things I have been making up excuses to avoid for years. I think maybe we're just too old for that stuff now." The husband, on the other hand, wanted nothing more than to "make up for lost time."

In other marriages, though the more outgoing partner may accommodate for a while, in the end the social phobia hurts the marriage. One newlywed husband commented to me with frustration, "I love her and I'm very proud of her. She's good looking and I want to show her off. I'm completely sick of staying home or going only to her parents' house. Is this a life? I need more." At some point, such couples "grow apart" and the tension over socializing is no longer tolerable. Socially outgoing partners may well grow intolerant of withdrawn spouses, but severely socially anxious people may stay in undesirable or less-than-desirable relationships rather than risking divorce and loneliness. "It wasn't the best," said one woman ruefully, "but it wasn't an empty room either. Although he yelled at me and criticized me for twenty-five years, the idea of having to reenter the social world put a stop to my fantasies about leaving him."

Caspi and colleagues, who researched the marriage patterns of the socially anxious, discovered that men with a history of shyness tended to find stable work later in life, and to delay marriage and having children. These men also measured somewhat lower in occupational stability and achievement and had higher probabilities of being divorced or separated. The reasons for these data, it is postulated, are that individuals who are "out of synch" in these ways must cope with the demands of their multiple roles without the benefit of those social or institutional structures that smooth the way for those who are on schedule—they lack, for example, friends at the same age and stage, career counselors, and so on.

Caspi and colleagues found that shy women, however, did not delay marriage or starting families. However, it is important to know in assessing these results that the subjects studied reached the age of majority during the late 1940s, a time when sex roles—particularly with respect to courtship—were much more traditional. At that time, as we all know, all women, not just shy ones, were much more likely than those coming of age today to lead a prototypical homemakers' life. Further, the majority of these women—56 percent—had no work history at all or terminated employment at marriage or childbirth and never re-entered the workforce.[26]

It seems possible that any long-term studies of women would have different outcomes now. At the time of Caspi's study, shyness was probably less of a handicap in finding a mate than it might be nowadays. As our society continues to grow more egalitarian and self-assertion is more fully incorporated into our common understanding of femininity, it is likely that women might be disproportionately handicapped by social anxiety than men, who have always been and continue to be supported by the social establishment and culture.

Chapter 6

Social Fear in Children

"But that isn't right. The King of Beasts shouldn't be a coward," said the Scarecrow.

"I know it," returned the Lion, wiping a tear from his eye with the tip of his paw. "It is my great sorrow, and makes my life very unhappy. But whenever there is danger, my heart begins to beat fast."

"Perhaps you have a heart disease," said the Tin Woodsman.

"It may be," said the Lion.

— L. Frank Baum, *The Wizard of Oz*

WHERE DOES IT COME FROM? How do people become so fearful of other people that their lives are attenuated and much of their potential lost? In preceding chapters we looked at some of the evolutionary logic that might account for the excessive fear of people in our species as a whole. Here I trace social anxiety back to its source in the individual, noting along the way how these two paths dovetail.

Many of my patients with social phobia recall an isolated childhood broken up by agonizing episodes of forced interaction with others. "I've been this way all my life," said Karen. At age twenty-nine, she had finally capitulated to her parents' urgings and came to our anxiety clinic. She was a bright, articulate young woman—but it should be mentioned that it was some time before she had gained the sense of trust and social ease to reflect on her biography in the way reported here. "They keep telling me that life is passing me by. But I *want* it to—I'm constantly nervous when there's anyone around. The only time I can feel relaxed is when I'm alone."

When I asked her to describe her childhood, she reported memories of this "nervousness" from at least the age of five, "and probably before that, but I can't remember any further back. My mother told me I was a 'clinger,' even as a little baby. I don't think I *ever* was in a room with other people, besides my parents, when I wasn't worried about what they were thinking about me and whether they'd start asking me questions I'd have to answer. My worst nightmare was that something would happen to cause me to be the center of attention. And it didn't help to be a redhead, because I blushed so badly I splotched."

"One awful day, one of the worst days of my life, my third-grade teacher saw my blotches and asked me in front of the whole class whether I was sick and needed to go home. I know it sounds like such a little thing, even a nice thing for her to do, but to me it was a catastrophe, my nightmare coming true. After that I pretended to my mother that I *was* sick, and I lied to get out of school whenever I could."

Social phobia in children is all but unstudied, and self-reports by patients are obviously colored by the subjective experiences being recounted. But when I have asked parents about their children's early years, they usually confirm the patients' recollections, adding examples of extreme social reticence, severe shyness, or stubborn childhood fears involving other people.

Still, though such anecdotal reports help us understand the subjective experience of social phobia from an intuitive point of view, no concrete markers arise in the childhoods of socially phobic adults that could serve as accurate predictors. In fact, it is difficult to distinguish any social abnormalities in the fearfulness or reticence that occurs naturally and for good reason during childhood development.

NORMAL FEARS IN INFANCY

Humans emerge from the womb having to learn from their parents and/or other significant adults around them not only motor skills—such as walking, talking, and tying their shoes—but social skills as well. Exploring normal human social development provides a fascinating context for looking at social phobia and speculating on its meaning in the evolutionary scheme. To keep this speculation on a human scale and prevent it from becoming an exercise in abstraction, I will sketch out the normal sequence of events as it unfolds in a real-life example. Let us call this healthy, well-balanced fellow, who is actually the child of friends of mine, Tim.

Tim was an even-tempered baby from the minute he was born. He cried when he was hungry, but not when he was wet, and instead of becoming cranky when he was tired, he simply fell asleep. He began to smile in his fourth week, and, although his grandmother attributed his happy facial expressions to nothing but gas, his young parents looked forward to an easygoing, untroubled first year.

Tim went without resistance to anyone who reached out for him, and he was often handed around at festive family gatherings. But at about six months of age, Tim seemed to undergo a personality change. If he lost sight of his mother, even for a moment, he shrieked and stiffened in apparent fear, visibly refusing comfort or distraction from concerned relatives with every muscle in his body. Likewise, if someone—even one of his many aunts and uncles—reached out to him, he screamed with apparent fear. When his mother returned and took him in her arms, Tim's sunny expression reemerged instantly, but his parents were concerned that unbeknownst to them someone had frightened their son and ruined his happy disposition.

The fact was, despite the apparent intensity of Tim's fear and his obvious distress, he was right on schedule for exhibiting and coming to grips with the two fear responses that characterize normal human infancy: *separation anxiety*, which is distress in response to the physical separation from the main caregiver, usually the mother; and *stranger anxiety, or wariness,* which occurs when the infant is exposed to unfamiliar people, usually adults.

Separation anxiety is perhaps the most studied of the two normal infant fears. It usually manifests itself at age six to seven months and becomes most intense near the end of the first year. Children experiencing this normal stage of development exhibit various signs of distress—crying, angry protest, and obvious search behaviors—when the mother or other central caregiver leaves their side.

After separation anxiety peaks, it gradually fades in the first months of the second year. We can interpret its disappearance as evidence of the baby's new understanding and trust, based on experience and learning, that the mother might go away but she will indeed return. And by extension, this change also suggests a new ability to conceptualize and understand abstractions—"she's not here now, but she always appears when I cry." The child weaves these concepts into the patchwork of reality that emerges as the human psyche matures. Although there is no empirical evidence to confirm the connection, it is of interest that many patients diagnosed in adulthood with panic disorder and agoraphobia showed evidence of excessive separation anxiety in childhood.

Stranger anxiety elicits similar reactions, but it occurs in response not to the caregiver's absence but rather to an unfamiliar person's presence. Typically, infants recognize a stranger *as* an unfamiliar person at approximately six months. We can assume that, despite our wishes to play a significant role in the worlds of our very young babies, in the earliest months everybody seems pretty much the same to them. The child does recognize its mother earlier and may even recognize strangers earlier, but wariness about strangers begins right on schedule between six and nine months of age. Once they gain the ability to recognize strangers as strangers, babies might be interested and friendly toward others while safe in their mother's arms, but if separated from the mother in the presence of the stranger, it is normal for them to be upset and even cry. At nine to twelve

months, babies show even more overt discomfort and fear in the
presence of strangers (usually adults, though other children can
evoke anxiety too), often avoiding eye contact with the stranger
and turning their bodies away, while clinging to the mother or
father. This fear usually wanes over the course of the second
year, but there is much individual variation. Without insisting
too heavily on the timetable, it is safe to predict that stranger
anxiety peaks between nine and twelve months, although some
observers have described a second peak of fearfulness between
eighteen and twenty-four months.

WHY ARE BABIES FEARFUL?

These two early fear responses, separation and stranger anxiety,
seem to be universal—they occur in all countries and all cultures. This suggests that the traits have a meaning for the human
species as a whole. As I have suggested earlier, attempts to interpret the "meaning" of various aspects of the human condition
consist of a great deal of observation followed by an equal
amount of educated guesswork. With regard to the meaning of
separation and stranger anxiety, the result is a raft of conflicting
theories. One popular view is rooted in theories of psychoanalysis. It holds that these two fears are related to the organization of
the human psyche, the development of the ego in the growing
infant, and the gradual experience of the self as distinct from
others. In brief, the psychoanalytic view suggests that until the
middle of the first year of life, the infant's perceived world is one
in which child and mother are merged, indistinct from each
other, a closed system of need and sustenance. With gradual
maturation comes a sense of an "I" that is separate and distinct
from the caregiver, a sense that the caregiver is distinct from anyone else. The psychodynamic researcher Rene Spitz, who performed a number of studies of separation on children in
orphanages, has argued that stranger anxiety suggests the emergence of a new level of organization of the psyche, the new abil-

ity to recall the image of the mother and compare it to the stranger.[1] So, in Spitz's view, Tim's fearful reactions would be interpreted as a sign of psychological maturation.

This traditional explanation is hotly defended by its advocates, but it was challenged by the pioneering developmental psychologist John Bowlby in his investigations into the evolutionary roots of maternal/infant attachment. Bowlby saw a survival value for both the individual and the species in separation and stranger anxiety, and I consider his point of view the more convincing and useful one. A human infant is a weak, defenseless creature, with barely the ability to discern its own caregiver, let alone to defend itself against danger. The infant's only hope of saving itself from a stranger intent on stealing it away or even eating it is to cry like hell—to scream—in the effort to draw attention to its predicament.[2]

From this point of view, separation from the caregiver and later, when brief separations are not necessarily life-threatening, the presence of strangers should trigger wariness, alarm, and finally full-blown fear—a condition that floods not only the psyche but the body with intense distress. Fear, in turn, triggers loud cries designed to attract the mother.

This response loop may have served in prehistoric times, and may serve to this day, to protect human infants from danger and increase their likelihood of surviving to adulthood. In the broadest view, the baby's fearful cry works to save not only itself but the whole human species—in that it contributes to the child's survival to reproductive age, when it can pass along its genetic material.

In support of this evolutionary view of infant fears, Isaac Marks, a British psychiatrist, regards the fear of strangers in human infants as an evolutionary "left-over" from a more brutish past, when strangers posed a very real danger to infants.[3] It is to be hoped that we have evolved as a species to a point where even infants separated from their watchful mothers or infants placed in the care of others are not generally at risk of being harmed or killed. But modern society being as complex, unpredictable, and

often violent as it is, who is to say that the normal infant fears are
not every bit as functional today as they were in prehistoric times
in keeping parents alert to outside dangers?

WHY FEARS RECEDE

These speculations become mere flights of fancy unless we consider how they play out in the individual. So, to return to our
example, by age three and a half, Tim's crying storms were over
and once again his parents could relax at the large, jovial family
gatherings that were traditional with them. At these parties and
picnics, they could once again feel confident that sociable Tim
would find a congenial cousin, aunt, or uncle to entertain or
play with him. He even became famous for stepping up to the
grumpiest stranger and beginning a conversation with a cheerful, "Hi, I'm Timmy."

So after three years of dreading social gatherings, where she
would have to endure Tim's clinging and fearful demands to be
carried, his mother finally began to relax again. She was famous
among her friends for her cooking, and now she and her husband gradually began to feel comfortable about extending their
hospitality.

During the normal course of development, as children enter
their third and fourth years, they begin to draw on the broad-
ened range of their experience. Not only have they collected
positive memories of social interactions with adults who are not
their parents, but their cognitive skills have improved to the
point where they can begin to distinguish potentially dangerous
situations from safe ones. This new ability to think things
through has some potential to override or conceal the biologically programmed social fears.

But even more influential—for better or worse—with respect
to the development of its newly emerging social skills is the
baby's observation of its parents' responses to strangers and
unfamiliar situations. For Tim's parents, socializing with family

and friends were a natural part of life even when Timmy's fears put a crimp in their style. For other parents, social gatherings might be a trial, a bore, or a terror. Whether or not parents' dislike or fear of socializing contributes to the development of social phobia in people who suffer from it we simply do not know.

But we do know that this "social referencing"—in which children learn from those around them how to respond to others—becomes more and more powerful as the child develops. It is by imitation that children learn, for example, how to carry on a conversation, when to look into another's eyes and when to look away, how close to stand, when it is all right to touch another, when to reassure another, how to signal interest, how to signal reassurance, how to end a conversation, how to share a meal with others—in short, the complex, often unspoken rules and rituals that govern human interaction within a specific culture.

There is much to learn, and a great deal of parenting is taken up in conveying "the way we do things" with respect to other people. By this I mean that perhaps even more important than individual "rules" is a general attitude about social interaction and how it should be conducted. In a child who is inadequately socialized, taught the dreaded possibilities of "social failure," or encouraged through social referencing to be inordinately wary of others, "failure" might actually exaggerate the inherent fear tendencies, causing them not to recede pretty much on schedule but rather to blossom as never before.

THE BEGINNINGS OF THE SELF

Clinicians who work regularly with children generally agree that it is between the ages of seven and nine that normal children begin developing a strong concept of self, a sense of themselves as social beings that tends to persist into adulthood. This growing awareness of themselves as distinct individuals can lead, overall, to a positive unfolding of personality traits, but at this developmental juncture social experience can have some distressing qualities as well.

For example, as awareness of self deepens, children become increasingly vulnerable to criticism, ridicule, and feelings of being "different," of not fitting in. Now, too, they become aware that others are observing, even scrutinizing them, and this knowledge begins to have an impact on self-esteem as children begin to include these factors in their own evaluations of their self-worth.

As we have seen social rituals—such as shaking hands, making nonthreatening eye contact, hugging or kissing in greeting, or simply approaching another open-handedly without even realizing it—are results of our "programmed" need to recognize and respond to others. With the help of social referencing to parents or other significant caregivers, at about the age of eight a child begins learning to read and send these subtle signals. In the process he or she gains a more clearly defined sense of individual self.

In attempting to understand social anxiety, it is interesting to note that whereas in normal children first fears are "overridden" by maturation and replaced with more sophisticated responses, in certain children a dawning awareness of others' scrutiny at the age of four or five brings blushing and a sense of embarrassment. In children of this age, these traits are viewed as abnormal, symptoms of a disorder loosely dubbed self-conscious shyness.[4]

I discuss shyness in detail in a later section, but it is of interest to speculate here on the meaning of this developmental wrinkle where it occurs. Just as the receding of fears signals maturation, self-conscious shyness might indicate the emergence of the child's new ability to think in symbolic or abstract terms. Perhaps children who display it are actually precocious in comparing others' perceptions of them to their own ideal selves. It is also possible—though certainly not confirmed—that children with very early social responses of this sort may be more likely to develop social anxieties and phobias as adults. However, to date the research investigating such a possible link is nonexistent.

ADOLESCENCE—STORMY WITH INTERMITTENT CLEARING

The normal developmental sequence leading to the awareness of self sets the stage for adolescence, during which self-consciousness becomes intensified by many degrees. To return to the example of my young friend Tim, at twelve the boy had a pretty fair social life of his own. Come the weekend, and he would call a friend from school or his baseball team to come over to play and spend the night. Even more gratifying to his parents were the frequent invitations Tim received to accompany his friends on their family excursions. People seemed to like Tim and he clearly liked them.

But there came a time for Tim—it was when he was fourteen, but there is a wide range during which this can occur—when everything on the social front that had once come easily suddenly seemed practically impossible. On weekends, he sat morosely for hours in front of the television set. Sometimes in late afternoon in the family room he would fall asleep on the couch and angrily fend off all efforts to wake him up until ten or eleven at night. Then he would stay up until the early mornings, gloomily watching more TV.

He and his best friend, with whom he had been exceptionally tight since the fifth grade, suddenly started having explosive arguments. These would erupt with no warning away from home, and Tim—too young to have a driver's license and apparently too angry and hurt even to wait for a ride home—would simply stomp off and make the four-mile walk home with his hands jammed into his pockets and a scowl on his once friendly face. After one such incident, during a sudden storm of tears and yelling, Tim's parents learned that the boys' arguments had something to do with girls. John had a girlfriend; Tim didn't. "I'm just a *dork, that's* why!" Tim shouted at his mother when she asked why that mattered at all. "*Nobody* wants to hang out with me. Look at my clothes. Look at my *room*—it's so stupid! Who would want to come over here? I'm just an *id*iot."

It seemed to Tim's parents that someone had spirited their friendly, open-faced boy away in the middle of the night, leaving a crabby, unpredictable look-alike in his place. "I've heard of teenage mood swings," commented Tim's dad, "but I never realized they set the whole family swinging. What have we done to make Tim so unbelievably self-conscious? What can we do to make him like himself?"

The answer to both questions, all else being normal, is nothing. Adolescence is a turbulent time because it is a transition in the normal developmental timetable. Puberty brings bodily, emotional, and cognitive cha ges, which in turn trigger changes in social roles and relationships, particularly within the family. In this phase, the developmental task that growing children perform is to begin to refine their thinking about themselves vis-à-vis others, to learn to "think about thinking," and to imagine other people's thoughts. Still, with these abilities in dealing with abstractions still so new, adolescents are often unable to distinguish between their own and others' interests. They become preoccupied with their behavior and appearance and, with the awareness that others are indeed perceiving and thinking about them, feel as though they are constantly on stage. The bodily changes associated with puberty only accentuate this feeling of being caught in the spotlight.

The operative phrase in the last paragraph is "all else being normal." For anxious parents attempting to help their children grow into psychologically and socially healthy adults, it becomes important to try to distinguish between the self-consciousness normal to adolescence and the kinds of shyness and extreme self-consciousness that may be the psychological forerunners of social phobia.

NORMAL SHYNESS

In 1896, Harry Campbell, a British physician, delivered a detailed report on what he termed "morbid shyness" to the British Medical Society. With literary flair, he described the shy person this way: "His soul is full of love and song, but the world knows it not; the iron mask of shyness is riveted before his face and the man beneath is never seen. Genial words and greetings are ever rising to his lips but they die away in unheard whispers before the steel clamps."[5]

As full of empathy as this description appears to be, for many years the scientific community showed remarkably little interest in shyness. Perhaps the shy and socially anxious were *too* successful in their attempts to remain unobtrusive and nearly invisible. Even though over the years terms such as *introversion, reticence, neuroticism,* and *withdrawal* were used to describe social distress, little research literature focused on the roots or dynamics of shyness itself. Perhaps, like the common cold, shyness has been mostly ignored because it is so very common.

But in the 1970s, science began to look at this elusive concept, and as the self-help movement surged during that decade, a variety of books appeared that espoused to the shy various ways of coping with their social discomforts. The writer most widely known for bringing shyness into the public light was Philip Zimbardo.[6]

In 1972, with colleagues, Zimbardo administered to more than 10,000 subjects the Stanford Shyness Survey. Forty percent of the subjects described themselves as shy in some sense. When asked whether they had *ever* viewed themselves as shy, 80 percent reported they had, 17 percent said they had never labeled themselves shy but felt they had had feelings of shyness in certain situations, and only 1 percent reported never having experienced shyness at all.[7]

Zimbardo and his colleagues also examined other cultures and countries. They found that, compared to Americans, the Japanese and Taiwanese had a greater percentage of shy people (60 percent of the total population); at 30 percent of the total, Israel had the lowest. And in no culture did more than 10 percent of the respondents describe themselves as "never shy." In attempting to define the vague subjective term "shyness" with some precision, Zimbardo and his colleagues provided us with a useful breakdown of its fundamental components in four realms of subjective experience:

- *Cognitions*—that is, thoughts, include perceptions of self-consciousness, concerns about impressions one is making on others, concerns about what others are thinking, and the person's own negative self-evaluations.
- *Affective states*, or shy feelings, include the awareness of anxiety, feelings of distress, nervousness, embarrassment, and awkwardness.
- *Physiological changes*, such as increased pulse rate, blushing, perspiration, palpitations, trouble breathing, and "butterflies in the stomach."
- *Behavioral responses*—among males, include diminished talking and diminished eye contact, compared with nonshy males; and among females, high frequencies of head nodding and nervous smiling.[8]

Besides describing the subjective experience of shyness, Zimbardo and his group surveyed the adverse consequences of shyness as described by their respondents. They reported that shyness creates social problems, making it difficult to meet people, make friends, or enjoy potentially good experiences. It is associated with unpleasant emotions such as depression, isolation, and loneliness. Shyness makes it hard to be assertive of or express personal opinions and values. It makes others view one negatively or fail to perceive one's personal assets. It causes a person to be judged—wrongly—as snobbish, unfriendly, bored, or weak. It interferes with clear thinking or communicating. And it causes one to be self-conscious and excessively concerned with others' reactions. In a poignant summation of the subjective experience of shyness, Zimbardo quotes several of his respondents in their eighties as longing "to enjoy one non-shy day before they die."

Zimbardo strongly believed that shyness was not a natural state that normal children grew out of but a significant psychological phenomenon "that can have profound effects upon many aspects of the shy person's life" and a significant personal problem of major proportions. Zimbardo's careful identification of the components of shyness and his description of its adverse consequences permit us to begin to see how shyness is related to social phobia and how to distinguish between them.[9]

SHYNESS AND SOCIAL PHOBIA

Although Zimbardo and others have described the adverse consequences and disabling behaviors associated with the experience of shyness, no one has attempted to measure the phenomenon. To shed light on this cloudy issue, it will help to view shyness as a psychological continuum affecting between 25 and 40 percent of Americans. Within this continuum, we can identify various levels of intensity and disability:

- The greatest proportion of those experiencing shyness fall into the *normal* range.
- About 8 percent of those reporting shyness are what some researchers term "borderline" cases—that is, sometimes disabled by their shyness and sometimes not. (Age has an impact too: over time shy people can become less so and nonshy people more so.)
- According to epidemiological research, approximately 2 percent of our population are socially phobic—that is, severe enough to cause social impairment.
- One more psychiatric category, called avoidant personality disorder, may represent the most disturbed extreme of the continuum.

When we view the continuum as a whole, it is easy to see why the word "shyness" is often used haphazardly by both lay and professional people. To clarify, shyness is a form of social anxiety, while generalized social phobia is a more extreme form. Because of the lack of clarity about these terms, even much of the empirical research on shyness actually focuses on social phobia.

Let us leave the laboratory and return to real life to get a feel for what these distinctions mean. At fourteen, Tim often felt too shy to ask a girl out on a date and even too shy—"like a dork," to use his words—to hang out with his childhood buddy and his girlfriend. Indeed, given Zimbardo's list, at his shyest, Tim would undoubtedly have checked off every single one of the adverse consequences Zimbardo identifies as being associated with shyness. In fact, if Tim had been diagnosed at the height of his difficulties, he might have been classified as socially phobic. However, Tim was destined to emerge from the transition out of childhood and to finish high school and go on to college with a renewed zest for social interaction—not to mention increasingly effective social sᴵ ls.

The fate of Annemarie, a patient at the anxiety clinic, was very different. In the history she recounted, she reported having blushed and experienced embarrassment at about six, and these symptoms increased throughout her school years until she was virtually mute throughout her adolescence. Her peers kept clear of her and her teachers considered her a problem; to protect her from her bouts of painful blushing and stammering that caused the whole class to become agitated, they tended to ignore her in class discussions.

"She did not finish high school because of her 'shyness,'" I wrote in my notes. "She stated that she was always a tense, nervous wreck all of the time. She was constantly sweating, her heart rate was consistently elevated, and she was fearful of every social interaction. She was especially fearful of talking in class and when called upon would mumble and decline, and hence, believed that the teachers thought she was stupid." She "had several friends but in high school would not engage in larger group activities, so she never really did anything with other people. She never went out on dates."

Annemarie quit school at sixteen, and despite her parents' relative affluence and their high hopes for her, she began cleaning houses for a living. They begged her to choose a vocation and offered to pay her tuition for any school, even to send her abroad, but the most she would promise was that she would get a high school graduation equivalency diploma. In the long run, though, she decided against even that. "What's the use? I wouldn't do anything else anyway. I *couldn't*."

Unquestionably, Annemarie's "shyness" was no passing phenomenon related wholly to adolescence. Its effects were as disabling as any chronic physical illness might have been—it was directly responsible for impairing her ability to function in the world. For those attempting to assess the shyness of a loved one and predict its course, the news is frustrating, for only in retrospect, when we look back at the course of an individual's development, are we able to distinguish between normal, transient shyness and crippling social phobia.

It is true that in children it is often difficult to know where variations of normal behavior end and serious psychiatric conditions begin. Although sometimes the best we can do is wait and see whether or not the "shyness" of a child or adolescent will fade or prove to be lasting and disabling, psychiatrists do have criteria for diagnosing disorders that impair social interaction in children. The questions they ask in assessing a child's fears and social behavior are these:

- Are their fears and behavioral signals excessive—that is, completely inappropriate to the situation?
- Are they completely beyond the child's voluntary control?
- Do they cause significant discomfort and notable avoidance behavior?

Using these criteria, child psychiatry has identified and described several common diagnosable social disorders that are found exclusively in children and that influence the development of social skills and comfort.[10]

COMMON DIAGNOSTIC SYNDROMES

In the past, social phobia was categorized strictly as a disorder of adulthood. Partly for historical reasons but partly because children's fears and symptoms differ from those of adults, child psychiatry has come up with other diagnoses to describe and identify childhood anxiety disorders. Some of these have similar features.

Overanxious disorder is characterized by excessive anxiety and fearful behavior that is not focused on specific situations. Children with this syndrome are "worriers," and they show anxiety about everything—academics, athletics, clothes, hair, their bodies, their past behavior, their future behavior, their siblings' and parents' behavior—in addition to matters involving other people. The mother of one such worrier, a boy of seven, characterized the extremity of the problem by reporting, "I've always hated lying, but from the very time that James learned to talk, I realized I'd have to keep many things from him or we would never get out of the house. Unless I can help it, I never tell him until we're about to leave where we are planning to go. If I let him know the day before, he literally wouldn't be able to sleep. Meals can be very difficult, because he is visibly anxious about almost anything that gets mentioned—Daddy losing his job, wars, riots, all kinds of things. School has become nearly impossible, because he worries about what might happen if he has to go to the bathroom and miss something that could turn out to be important. He broods about things like that in bed every school night, thinking about things—little things that most people would never give a thought to—and by the next day he's worried to death." In summary, overanxious disorder is characterized by undifferentiated anxiety about *many* different things and does not focus particularly on social or evaluative kinds of worries.

Childhood *separation anxiety* is an extreme and persistent version of normal separation fears that last beyond the expected developmental period in the first and second years of life. Typically, children diagnosed with this syndrome worry about harm coming to themselves or their families during their absences from home. In one example, eight-year-old Lynda became adept at convincing adults that she was ill, with nausea and stomach cramps, and often had to leave school and, in the summer, day camp. Both her parents worked, and these frequent "cries of wolf" were not only troubling but highly disruptive to their work lives. Lynda's mother was pretty sure that

Lynda was not sick but took her to a pediatrician for a full physical. As expected, the doctor found nothing.

Then the family went on a search together to find an overnight camp for Lynda—she was enticed by the horses to look forward to going to camp herself. But once there, she began to report to the infirmary every morning with nausea and stomach cramps. Finally, the camp directors asked Lynda's parents to come and get her, and when they arrived, Lynda burst into relieved hysterics at the sight of her mother. "I thought you died," she finally admitted. "I thought you sent me to camp so you could have an operation and you died in the hospital."

"But who did you think was sending you all those letters in my handwriting?"

"I didn't know—" cried the girl. "And that scared me even more."

Children with separation anxiety—fearing separation, not interactions with others—often complain of physical symptoms to avoid school or sleeping away from home. This disorder may be related to or even an early manifestation of panic disorder and agoraphobia in adulthood.

Of the currently recognized childhood anxiety disorders, *avoidant disorder* seems closest to adult social phobia. This disorder is characterized by excessive anxiety over social contact with unfamiliar people—anxiety extreme enough to interfere with peer relationships. And yet, the child generally wants to have social contact and—like most adult social phobics—is able to relate well to familiar people such as family members. Here again the problem becomes *when* to diagnose a disorder. The diagnosis has to be delayed unless and until the symptoms persist after the normal period for stranger anxiety. It typically appears during the early school years but may occur as early as two and a half to three years.

Finally, *school phobia* or *school refusal* arise frequently in the context of childhood anxiety. These are actually general, descriptive terms pertaining to behavior rather than specific diagnoses. Any of the diagnoses just described may cause children to refuse to go to school. Increasingly, as a reflection of the growing familiarity with social anxiety as a discrete phenomenon, when faced with this behavior in their young clients, clinicians are attempting to distinguish between the fear of being away from home and parents and the fear of interacting with other people.[11]

It is important to emphasize that all of these disorders can overlap with each other, and all may contain some aspects of shyness or social anxiety. I cite them here to emphasize the difficulty of categorizing human behavior—especially that of children and adolescents, when rapid change is the rule. As is true for every psychological assessment and psychiatric diagnosis, it is essential to take account of the forest as well as the trees.

INHIBITED CHILDREN

Diagnostic categories in children have not been well studied over time, so we do not know which of these conditions continue into adulthood or which, if any, become social phobia. But some answers about the course of these conditions might come from an ambitious investigation into social inhibition by the Harvard psychologist Jerome Kagan and his colleagues.

Kagan's prior work had indicated that about 10 to 15 percent of healthy two- and three-year-old children consistently became quiet, vigilant, and subdued when faced with unfamiliar events and especially unfamiliar people, while an equal proportion appeared to treat the distinctions between familiar and unfamiliar as unimportant.[12] Interestingly, these patterns—extreme attentiveness to and extreme disinterest in unfamiliarity—are reflected in many other species, and in a similar proportion. In more recent studies the investigators looked at a total sample of 400 toddlers. Culling out the extremes on each end as separate categories, they called the most spontaneous *uninhibited* and the least spontaneous and most fearful, *inhibited*.[13]

Kagan filmed the children in these two groups in unfamiliar

rooms with unfamiliar people and objects over a series of years; he also filmed them in their own homes during the same period. Compared to the "average child," who was sometimes subdued, sometimes not, the group he called inhibited "went to their mothers right away" when faced with an unfamiliar person or place. "They became very quiet, they stopped playing—sometimes for three minutes, sometimes for five. And then they ventured forth. And they did that in every single situation." The uninhibited group were just the opposite and equally consistent. "They rush up to the stranger, they smile, they laugh, and they *never* go to their mothers."

Having grouped their subjects, Kagan and his colleagues tracked these children over time. Briefly, these were their findings:

- At twenty-one to thirty-one months, the uninhibited group quickly entered into play or conversation with both unfamiliar children and adults, while the inhibited group showed withdrawal, clinging, crying, slow approach time, inhibited play, expressions of distress, and elevated heart and respiration rates.
- At about the age of three, the uninhibited children remained spontaneous. The inhibited children were still distressed in all unfamiliar situations, but were showing the most distress in the presence of unfamiliar peers.
- At ages four through six, the uninhibited remained so, while as a group the inhibited showed more marked distress around others and a new anxiety about how others saw and judged them. According to their mothers, this group also had more fears, nightmares, sleeplessness, allergies, and constipation.
- At the age of five and a half, 78 percent of the original inhibited group remained in that category. In play with unfamiliar peers and in their own school settings, these children talked and interacted with other children measurably less than the uninhibited groups.
- Six years after the start of the study, when the children were seven and a half, approximately 75 percent of those who had initially been observed to be extremely timid and inhibited

were still quiet and socially introverted with unfamiliar children and an unfamiliar examiner.
- Throughout the course of the six-year study, the inhibited children had markedly higher heart rates, muscle tension of the
larynx and vocal cords, and other physiological evidence of the
response of the sympathetic nervous system to stress.
- And, tantalizingly, blue-eyed children were found to be more
likely to be shy than brown-eyed children, suggesting the possibility of a genetic influence on level of social ease.[14]

The consistency of social inhibition and the associated physiological measurements led Kagan to theorize that inhibited children are *born with* a nervous system more easily aroused by
changes in the environment. With regard to the physiological
changes, Kagan believed that, compared with uninhibited children, inhibited children had lower thresholds of excitability in
the limbic structures of the brain, structures located deep within
the part of the brain commonly considered to be the site of the
production of emotion. But he also noted that some of the physiological differences between inhibited and uninhibited children became less extreme by the age of seven and a half. It thus
appeared that as growing children cope with new stressors, physiological variables such as heart rate and levels of the stress hor-
mone cortisol become less sensitive signs of disturbance.
Perhaps, he speculated, social inhibition is to some degree
inherited but influenced as well by an habituation to social interaction.[15]

Since then, substantial empirical evidence has accrued—
especially from comparisons of twins—to confirm that shyness,
or social inhibition, has genetic roots. In fact, the evidence
shows that of all the personality traits, shyness appears to have
the strongest genetic component. Further, where extreme shyness is present, most studies suggest that some sort of biological
vulnerability or anxiety proneness is passed on genetically.[16]
However, although the empirical evidence *tends* toward that conclusion, we cannot interpret these results as "proof" that shyness

is inherited. Many other factors influence human behavior, and each one can have a profound effect that is beyond our ability to measure in a laboratory. Let us look at each of these factors in turn.

SOCIAL BEHAVIOR LEARNED IN THE HOME

Even very young children are likely to pick up cues from a parent who is anxious in the presence of others. It is not unusual, in interviewing the parents of young anxiety patients, to hear, for example, that Mom usually takes a few drinks *before* going to a party or Dad has never been much of a "people person" and so never used his law degree but became a bookkeeper instead.

Also, some investigators have suggested that the parents of socially phobic children may place excessive emphasis on the importance of proper grooming, dress, manners, and social decorum.[17] Instead of inviting friends and acquaintances into the home and encouraging their children to do likewise, these parents might be continually reminding their children, explicitly or implicitly, that others are examining and judging their appearance and behaviors. Further evidence points to the possibility that shy mothers might perpetuate a cycle of social fear by keeping themselves and their children away from anxiety-inspiring social events.

Many socially phobic people perceive their parents as both overprotective and undersupportive. "My mother distrusted everybody," reported Annemarie. "She was always at me to tell her what people said or how they treated me—especially teachers and other people in authority. And when she heard something she didn't like, she'd kind of fly off the handle. 'Nobody talks to my daughter like that!' 'Who does that bastard think he is?' That kind of thing. But she never went down to the school to complain. And she never really asked how *I* felt about it. Once or twice she got really bent out of shape about something my favorite teacher said to me. If it hadn't been for this woman I don't think I would have made it as far as I did in high school, but my mother practically had a tantrum because she thought the teacher was 'uppity.' I guess I probably stopped telling my mom pretty early about the things that were really bothering me in school. She worried more about whether I would do something wrong and embarrass myself than I did myself. And I don't think she would have heard me if I talked to her about my deepest concerns. She was always too wrapped up in what people would think."

Some patients forthrightly accused their parents of rejecting them, but reports of this sort have to be interpreted with caution.[18] Not only is such a memory corrupted by the passage of time, but it may also reflect the person's own needs or subconscious wishes. A psychotherapist or other care provider needs to learn a great deal about the psychological dynamics of the family before interpreting the meaning or judging the veracity of such a recollection.

For example, children with a low arousal threshold for anxiety who are constantly stressed by changes in the social environment may make such high demands on parents for nurturing and support that they may be difficult to satisfy. Children with an intense need for approval might perceive their parents as rejecting when in fact their responses fluctuate as in any normal household. Finally, an anxious person's feeling of being rejected, whether based in reality or not, could lead to or reinforce a preoccupation with others' evaluations. For example, Annemarie's extreme discomfort in the presence of others could well be traced back to her mother's intense fear of judgment or criticism.

CHILDHOOD ILLNESS

In investigating the roots of social anxiety in children, some researchers have pointed to an as yet unexplained association between shyness and childhood illness. In one 1986 study, children who were currently or previously shy were more likely to report stomach ailments, sleep disturbances, headaches, and allergies than those who were never shy.[19] A large study in 1990 found that most young adults who fell into the "introverted" category had more hay fever than nonintroverted respondents.[20] If these findings are valid and if there is a causative connection between childhood illness and social anxiety, it is interesting to speculate on which, if either, is the causative agent, the illness or the social anxiety. A third, perhaps genetic factor may cause both conditions.

BIRTH ORDER

Another possible factor in social anxiety is birth order. Several studies have found that only children—children with no siblings—are most shy, followed by first-born siblings. Last-born siblings are least shy.[21] These findings suggest that the presence of siblings gives children an opportunity to practice social skills and thus become less inhibited.

However, socially anxious and socially phobic people are not generally—and certainly not necessarily—deficient in social skills. George is typical. "The thing is, I have a pretty good sense of humor," he told me. "My wife and daughters think so, anyway. But it deserts me when I most need it—I could really use it to lighten up my relationship with my co-workers. They think I'm a dud. And when I'm with them I *am* a dud. But at work my mind gets so muddled I can hardly say my name, let alone toss off a joke or tease somebody. It's really frustrating to know I'm an okay guy and yet every day come off so formal and straight-laced and nervous at the office."

George, the only child of two hardworking shopkeepers, was happily married and had good relationships with both of his daughters. But outside the family, George "turned into a different person." It was the frustration of coping with this Jekyll/Hyde phenomenon that finally brought him into the clinic.

Finally, although the studies cited suggest that the presence of older siblings has a *positive* effect, Kagan's long-term studies of childhood inhibition yielded mixed messages: two-thirds of the inhibited children were born later, but two-thirds of the *uninhibited* children were first-borns. This stalemate leads to the possibility that, rather than having a positive effect on social comfort, the presence of an older sibling who torments or teases a younger child, especially a younger child with a low threshold for autonomic arousal, could be an ever-present negative force, enough to transform a temperamental tendency into inhibited behavior.

In a sense, then, contemporary research only underscores the importance of proceeding cautiously and trying to differentiate between those children who are quiet, restrained, and inhibited owing to inherited traits of temperament, and those who may be pushed in this direction by experiences in their families and the outside world.

IF YOUR CHILD HAS SOCIAL ANXIETY

Since I have become known for my work with socially phobic patients, I find that when I go to a party, sooner or later someone expresses concern about a highly inhibited, socially anxious child or other relative. I devote a later chapter exclusively to the diagnosis and treatment of social phobia in adults, but for those parents who may be seeking solutions to a painful family puzzle—"what's wrong with my child and what can I do to help?"—I digress here to respond briefly. Concerned parents seeking answers about children on the extreme end of the shyness continuum may be disappointed with the contradictory conclusions reported in the psychological and psychiatric literature. Often, parents show as much if not more acute distress as the patients themselves about the effects of their children's condition on quality of life. "Her life is so *small*," said one father of a young woman who, like Annemarie, had become a housecleaner. "That girl could have done whatever she wanted to do—she was gifted. I just can't understand how she could throw it all away just because she's shy." His disappointment was keen. "If those people knew who was cleaning their houses, if they *knew*—"

My answer to parents is, try to take a balanced view rooted in common sense. It is not easy to understand what is happening with our children, especially in the outside world. Some parents, seeing their child engaging in friendly, lighthearted interactions with family members and perhaps bringing home good grades, might not realize that at school or in other situations with peers the child is isolated and suffering. Others might tend to deny the significance of what they see—the child is only "a little shy" (this reaction is especially common among parents of girls), "going through a stage," "more interested in intellectual pursuits." "She'll grow out of it," they say to themselves and to each other.

But sometimes the children don't grow out of it. Staying alert to what is really going on may require self-discipline, patience, and some gentle probing. Ask yourself: are there warning signs that might indicate a fear of social interaction—for example, overinvolvement with television, computers, video games, and hobbies? Are there frequent excuses to avoid social engagements, such as unexplained physical complaints (headaches, stomach aches, "feeling sick to the stomach")?

If you do decide that your child is among the 15 percent of people occupying the "extreme" end of the spectrum, don't panic. Above all, it is important that you avoid labeling the child, communicating your concern, and setting up expectations in your own mind or the child's. Many patients have reported that "I never thought of myself as different until my parents started referring to me as 'the shy one.'" Such labels are easily incorporated into a child's self-image.

Next, expect to do a certain amount of self-introspection, again requiring honesty and a sincere effort to see your family life with fresh eyes. Remember that children appear to be at increased risk for disabling social anxiety if their parents have anxiety conditions of their own. Ask yourself:

- Do I have symptoms of extreme anxiety, especially social anxiety?
- Am I overprotecting my child or keeping myself socially isolated and unavailable owing to fears of my own? For example, do you allow the child to hang back from engaging in introductions? Do you easily accept "excuses" to avoid situations—say, by allowing your child to sit with you at social gatherings rather than interacting with other children? Do you make excuses so your child can avoid birthday parties or other situations where you know he or she will be uncomfortable? Do you drive your child places in order to avoid carpooling with other children?
- Can you identify self-protective measures in yourself—for example, a consistent reluctance to attend social functions, a long-standing refusal to invite outsiders into your home, a tendency to emphasize negative judgmental qualities of others—that might undermine your child's self-confidence and natural development toward independence? If so, it would bring your child relief if you discussed forthrightly these experiences and your means of handling them.

As to how to understand your child's social anxiety, in a general sense it might be helpful to think of him or her as having been born with a particularly sensitive or arousable nervous system that might cause a child to need particularly focused forms of support and guidance in entering the social arena. Not only might you need to respond with extra support, encouragement, and "practices" in which you participate in social activities together, but the child might require some active "coaching" and planning for specific situations.

Are the child's anxieties focused on the classroom? Address the problem head-on, talking out possible scenarios and stumbling blocks, and even coming up with a script or two for the kinds of encounters the child fears most. Practice alone will not resolve the symptoms of social phobia, but giving your child all possible tools for coping with difficult situations while expressing your concern on the problem can help to alleviate the feeling of bewildered isolation that troubled children inevitably feel.

There are trouble spots you can anticipate, such as being called on in class, needing to ask for a hall pass, being singled out for praise or criticism. As an example, consider the following script:

Tommy [clearly troubled]: I hate school. I hate lunch the worst.

Mom: You hate lunch? Why?

Tommy: Because the kids come up to me and I don't know what to say.

Mom: What about talking to them about the Green Bay Packers?

Tommy: I don't know what to say.

Mom: You know, people love questions. Maybe try asking, "Do you like the Packers? Have you ever gone to see them? Who is your favorite player?" I bet you'll get an answer.

Tommy: But what if they just say no?

Mom: Well, people love compliments too, even little ones. What about saying, "Hey, I like that lunchbox. Where'd you get it?" Or "I really like your haircut. I want to ask my mom to take me to get one like that." That might work with the really way-out kids.

Tommy: Yeah, they're the scariest ones.

Mom: Another thing you can do is ask about homework. Lots of people like to help people out, but only if they really *can* help. It probably wouldn't be good to ask the worst student about homework, but I bet that's a question the best student in your class would like to answer. Maybe the worst student is good at something else—like skating or drawing. You could ask about that.

For older children, the coaching can be more general, but the goal is still to demonstrate that social interaction consists of questions, voiced opinions, stated facts, and perhaps compliments. Practicing examples of each of these can help to reduce the child's sense of having no control. And modeling—actively putting to use the points you explain—can help to set the child at ease about needing help. "You know, I never used to know what to say to Harriet. She always seemed so intellectual to me, and I'm always afraid I'll sound dumb. But then I discovered that she loves compliments. Watch this—" Or, "Uncle Carl loves movies. Why don't you ask him whether he saw that movie you liked so much about the fugitive?" In this way, the child begins to learn that there is no mysterious code to social encounters that everyone else is privy to—a common misperception among the socially anxious. Be aware that a child with extreme anxiety, even if he or she "knows the rules of social interaction," may be helpless to find a way out of the loneliness and fear that characterize the existence of a social phobic. With support and affection, urge the child to join groups, if only as a silent observer, and above all to accompany *you* in similar settings. Using understanding, reassurance, and positive reinforcement, urge the child toward positive social experiences that might override his or her genetic tendencies and sensitive physiology.

Parents can deepen and broaden this home approach by engaging the participation of the child's teachers and other adults with whom the child regularly interacts. By identifying the child's social anxieties and attempting to foster a sense of acceptance and belonging, teachers may be able to keep the classroom from reinforcing the inherent social inhibition.

These suggestions are as much common sense as expert opinion—although in no way diminished by being so. For a more detailed approach to the clinical diagnosis and treatment of social phobia, see chapter 10.

Chapter 7

Seeing . . . and Being Seen

She would feel the first clutch of fear at the heart, as physical as pain, and then it would begin, the burning flush spreading over her neck, mottling her face and forehead, a scarlet deformity of shame. She felt every eye in the . . . room was fixed on her . . . stolidly gazing at her with their dead, controlled faces.
—P. D. James, *Innocent Blood*

R UNNING THROUGH THE ROOTS of social phobia, both evolutionary and developmental, and through the hundreds of therapy sessions in which I have treated socially phobic patients, is a single thread: the human gaze. Acute concern as to both how to react to the gaze of others as well as how to control one's own eyes—where and when to look and for how long—lies at the very heart of social phobia.

THE POWER OF EYES

Two staring eyes—the image is so potent that even the descriptive phrase seems eerie. And it is not just human beings who respond to it. Throughout the animal kingdom, eyes and their signals have forceful meanings. Eyes send messages not only across the boundaries of languages but even across those of species.

The meaning conveyed by the image of two staring eyes is found throughout nature—butterflies, fish, birds, and mammals all respond to it with fear, and numerous experiments have shown that paired-circle designs similar to eyes cause alarm. One study observed the effects of circular patterns on feeding birds—the more the circles resembled eyes, the more effective they were in provoking escape behavior.[1] This laboratory finding took on life-saving proportions in India, where villagers under repeated attack—from behind—by marauding Bengal tigers took to wearing face masks with prominent eyes on the back of their heads, thereby significantly increasing their life expectancy.

Humans are no less responsive to the power of eyes than are other organisms. Eyes are the first figures that infants discern, and two eyes appear to be all that is needed in the way of a visual cue to elicit a baby's smile, the first social response. Throughout the world, we can find our inherent fascination with eyes reflected in the art of children: the image of two staring eyes is the most common image found in their paintings and drawings.

But eyes lose none of their power and significance for us as we mature. Most people would intuitively agree that images of eyes are found everywhere throughout mythology, religion, the arts, folklore, and other manifestations of culture, but we come a bit closer to quantifying the human fascination with eyes when we note that the entries on "eyes" in *Bartlett's Familiar Quotations* are four times more numerous than those for "mouth."[2] In fact, a word count of normal conversation shows that the word "eyes" occurs more frequently than words denoting any other body part.[3]

Although we may be deeply involved in conversations of politics, aesthetics, baseball, any of a million engaging topics, it is safe to say that we maintain an awareness of the eyes of the people with whom we interact. Whether or not we are accurately interpreting the subtle, silent ocular signals sent over the course of a conversation or other social interaction, we are alert, watching, recording changes in the eyes of "the other," as those eyes are most certainly responding to our own.

EYE CONTACT

Prolonged, uninterrupted staring is disconcerting to everyone. In fact, a gaze that is unrelieved by occasional glances away, and changes, read as alterations in expression, around the eyelids, have occasionally been associated in the psychological literature with psychopathy and antisocial behavior. Such an uninterrupted gaze has even been named, tellingly, the "reptilian stare." Snakes are one of our archetypes of evil, and by association it is implied that a human being with a "reptilian stare" is a conscienceless individual with a fundamentally evil nature. Hollywood has used this concept to great effect, and more than one actor—Peter Lorre as the child murderer in the classic film *M* is a case in point—has boosted his career by perfecting the unrelieved, unblinking gaze.

There is good reason for our discomfort in the presence of the unmoving stare. In many species, eye contact is a mechanism employed for threatening purposes—in fact, researchers have been able to accurately predict the place in the social hierarchy of individual animals by studying the eye behaviors between dominant and subordinate animals.

In his memorable book *The Mountain Gorilla,* George Schaller recounts learning this lesson indelibly from his interactions with the lowland mountains gorillas of East Africa. In his attempts to accustom these mighty, overwhelmingly physical (though basically peaceful) creatures to his presence, Schaller discerned that direct eye contact was a challenging signal that provoked agitation and even aggressive displays of dominance. He soon learned never to approach a gorilla or a gorilla group without slowly turning his head from side to side, meeting the eyes of individuals only briefly and then breaking the gaze.[4]

Likewise, there is ample evidence that the language of the eyes reveals the distribution of power in the social relationships between humans. In both humans and primates in general, in struggles for dominance the direct stare is used as a threat. One researcher provided fascinating documentation on the subtle language of power expressed by minute changes in the gaze. Working with a territorial gang on Chicago's West Side, he found a "looking order" in the group that correlated with the dominance hierarchy. The rule was that attention was to be paid to the leadership, and to receive visual attention one had to earn it. The leaders never looked at the lower-status males, and although the subordinates constantly watched the leaders, they did not stare into the eyes of the dominant males. The researcher characterized the subordinates' behavior as "fearful watchfulness" and the dominants' behavior as expressive of "disdain." By noting who looked at whom, this investigator was able to construct a hierarchy that precisely matched members' ratings of one another's power within the group.[5] As noted previously, teachers learn to control their classrooms by sheer eye power alone, and parents are highly tuned into eye messages from their children that might be interpreted as naughty, critical, or "fresh."

In fact, in the whole animal realm, the sight of two eyes directed at us is a powerful trigger for response. Staring *demands* a response, and when a person being stared at finds no appropriate way to respond—or none that seems safe—tension and an anxiety to escape are the natural result.[6]

Charles Darwin believed that facial expressions were universal and that eye behavior is an integral part of facial expression. This notion has been debated for years, but the weight of the research at this point supports a cross-cultural universality for some expressions of emotion. The context, however, and the consequences of the behavior are altered by individual experiences and by cultural norms. Others assert that eye-movement expression is instinctual, not learned. The fact that these behaviors may be innate—that is, neurologically based—is important, because hereditary differences may cause tendencies toward abnormal eye behaviors, in performing, interpreting, and responding to eye behaviors. We know that there are specific cells or clusters located in the amygdala, a portion of the brain associated with emotions, specifically designed to "read" emotional expressions from others—specifically eye behaviors—and to implement responses.

As a measure of the extreme subtlety of the ocular language, just a few minute changes—Schaller's head-turning, for example—can change the meaning of the gaze from threatening to delightfully flattering, nurturing, even thrilling. In fact, except in encounters with real or Hollywood-crafted psychopaths, most of us not only deal effectively with eye contact but welcome it in social encounters. We feel cheated and eventually suspicious if a person is unable to "look us in the eye." The question is, cheated of what? We sense that we learn from the eyes of others, but precisely what information do we seek and find there?

With respect to the "language" of eyes—that is, the explicit meanings minute changes in the eyes hold for our species—research suggests that a direct gaze (distinct from the unbroken, threatening stare) carries one of two major meanings for humans. When we like someone, we tend to perceive their gaze as an indication of their interest and even affection. Conversely, when they avert their eyes, we feel less liked and like them less in return.[7] Eye contact is also used to intensify friendly feelings—if what a person says is friendly, eye contact makes it more so. The psychologist Paul Ekman, who has studied the meanings of facial expressions, describes the combination of movements that goes into an expression of flirtatiousness: the person looks away, then steals a glance at the person of interest, and then shifts the glance away again, with all three phases accompanied by a smile.[8] Ekman explains our perennial fascination with Leonardo da Vinci's *Mona Lisa* by citing it as the classic example of this flirtatious signal of interest. She faces one way but glances sideways and smiles at the object of her interest.

In his studies of human facial expression, Ekman reports that five kinds of changes around the human eyes convey the meaning we read there: changes in the muscles surrounding the eyeballs, the direction of the gaze, blinking, pupil dilation, and tear production. In these five tiny motions lies an entire dictionary of silent messages.[9]

SPEAKING WITH THE EYES

In precisely the same way that word formulas serve as rituals, certain sequences of eye behavior link to form normal, expected patterns. When eye patterns deviate from the norm of a particular cultural group, most people are likely to notice and to judge the person as abnormal or "strange." For example, in our culture, listening people look at the faces of speakers more often and for a longer duration than speakers look at listeners. In fact, speakers make direct eye contact the least, tending to look up briefly and only fixing the listener with a prolonged gaze upon finishing the spoken message.

A 1973 study of conversations found that in most two-party conversations each conversant looked at the other between 30 and 60 percent of the time. Glances during the conversations varied in length from about one to about seven seconds in length. When both conversationalists' eyes met—between 10 and 30 percent of the total time spent in conversation—they did so for about a second.[10]

These measurements can more or less be considered norms in the United States, but norms are greatly affected by other factors in the encounter. Position in the dominance hierarchy is one significant influence on duration of direct gazes in conversation. Dominant people seem to look more at others than submissive people, but this is not always true. In some situations, power resides with the one who looks back the *least* during listening. Apparently, the superior individual needs to pay less attention to the speaking behavior of the subordinate than vice versa; the more powerful person may spend up to 50 percent less time looking while listening.[11]

Culture affects the gaze norms, too, as most people are at least intuitively aware. For example, in the United States a person who looks "too long" conveys intimacy or a power challenge; one who looks too briefly suggests disinterest, dishonesty, or suspiciousness.[12] However, Arabs, Latin Americans, and southern Europeans focus their gazes on the eyes or faces of their conversants with far greater consistency than Americans do—for example, a pair of Arab conversants look at each other much more than two American or two English conversants would without signaling disrespect, threat, power assertion, or an interest in intimacy.[13] On the other hand, Japanese people orient themselves toward others without looking into their conversants' faces or eyes at all. From birth on, they are socialized to look at the neck in conversations and to look into the faces of superiors as little as possible.

Gender differences, too, shape eye behavior. For example, both females and males tend to look at members of their *own* sex more than at those of the opposite sex. And female pairs seem to spend more time in mutual gazes and mutual monitoring of facial expressions than do male pairs—in fact, women tend to engage in more eye contact than men in general and to look more, regardless of the sex of the people with whom they are interacting. However, although women look more, they usually modify their looking behaviors with submissive gestures—for example, looking away or looking down frequently to break eye contact. By comparison, men are more likely to use a direct and unbroken gaze.

Men and women also differ in their willingness to violate "personal space"—that is, to look directly at people whose gaze is averted from them.[14] In an experiment that required men and women to gaze at a range of people entering an elevator, women seemed to find men's looks to be threatening and seemed more willing to look at women, even women who were not looking back, than to gaze at men. Men, on the other hand, seemed *less* sensitive to gender, and seemed equally willing to gaze at anyone, regardless of gender. Whether or not these differences are inherent to the sexes or are the result of subverbal sex-role socialization we simply do not know.

SOCIAL PHOBIA AND THE LANGUAGE OF THE EYES

Given the subtlety and range of these signals and the fundamental information they relate, it is not surprising that people who experience high social anxiety share a deep concern, and often confusion, as to how to send and interpret such signals. As I mentioned earlier, I can reliably identify socially phobic patients in our clinic before they ever say a word. These patients make little or no eye contact with me during our initial greetings, and once in session inside my office they rarely if ever glance in my direction when they speak, only casting an occasional look my way when I am speaking.

"People are always saying to me, 'I'm here, not over there,'" said one woman, embarrassed by her inability to "get her eyes right." "I need to keep reminding myself to make eye contact," she said. "Sometimes I try to tell myself that the other person won't notice, but eventually I get it that they *do* notice." Indeed they do. Whether or not we are consciously aware of it, we are continually monitoring the eyes of others, and our sensitivity to eye signals is amazingly subtle. Try having a sustained conversation with somebody wearing opaque sunglasses and you will see what I mean. By the same token, try to talk with someone while never looking at them—you will quickly crave the reassurance conveyed by eye signals that your conversant is still engaged in the conversation.

My patients know that their ocular reticence is noticeable. "I'm constantly telling myself to make eye contact," they say, quickly adding, "and yet I feel so uncomfortable meeting someone's eye I just can't keep it up." When I press them on the source of the discomfort, the responses are usually generalities:

- I've always had this trouble.
- I'm just shy.
- It's just a habit.
- I don't know how to look at people.

The last response is the most interesting to me, as it suggests semiconscious awareness of the significant meaning of eye behaviors.

One of my patients who worked in a large corporation recounted his near obsession with "getting it right" as he walked through the corridors of his workplace. "I'm so anxious about it. When do I look up? When should I look away? I'm really afraid if I look too long that I seem to be coming off too fierce, too scary. And then I start worrying that I'm not looking long enough, and I'm coming off hostile and unfriendly." His nervousness about eye contact was—as he put it—driving him crazy. This is a striking example of how a seemingly small source of psychological distress can cycle into an overwhelming problem.

BEING WATCHED

Although I have never conducted a word count of my social phobics' conversations, I am fascinated by the frequency with which these patients refer to eyes, eye contact, and the experience of being watched. Socially anxious people suffer from an exaggeration of normal and common human propensities—they are hypersensitive to and sometimes preoccupied with the meaning of the language of the eyes.

One woman told me that she was unable to operate the computer under scrutiny; another person was inhibited from walking in certain parts of the city out of the fear of being seen to stumble and fall. A man was unable to perform on the job at all in the presence of others who might witness his work; he moved to the night shift to escape the staring eyes. It is important to realize that these social phobics are not simply concerned that their performance will evoke criticism—as all of us are at one time or another and especially on the job. This, indeed, is *part* of their discomfort at being watched, but in our sessions they tell me that there is something far more basic about being watched that accounts for their anxiety. "It's not what they might say or even think. It's just that I *cannot stand* to be stared at." I have heard this remark or versions of it from people explaining near paralysis when faced with having to stand up for weddings, take communion, walk through crowded meetings, enter a room after others have been seated, or even pass out leaflets to people who could be expected to welcome them.

Although never focused on socially phobic individuals specifically, many studies have examined the effects of being looked at. In general, this research demonstrates that for *all* of us, not just socially anxious people, being looked at causes arousal—it results in increases in heart rate, galvanic skin response (a measurable change in the temperature of the skin that is associated with arousal), and brain changes that can be measured on an electroencephalogram. This arousal, which in certain settings can be a form of discomfort, actually causes a response—that is, it provokes behavior.

But being looked at is even more powerful than a simple response trigger. Research shows that it can actually change behavior in the person being observed. In one social psychology experiment, a researcher posing as a bystander stared at some drivers who had stopped at a red light and gave other drivers a quick, inattentive glance. When the light changed, those who had been stared at pulled away faster than those who had merely been glanced at.[15]

In another experiment, a female member of the research team with her arms full of packages stood on a street corner and stared across the street at pedestrians waiting to cross. The pedestrian targeted by the woman's stare crossed more quickly than those who were not stared at. However, if the woman dropped a package while she stared at the person she singled out with her eyes, the targeted person was likely to approach, retrieve the package, and hand it to her. Dropping the package appears to have changed the meaning of the stare from threatening or disturbing to appealing.[16]

Although no research has focused on socially anxious people in particular, their own experiences suggest that social phobics are extremely susceptible to the power of others' gazes. They appear to experience the physiological arousal associated with being looked at more acutely, and the need to respond more urgently, than normal people. That they are exquisitely sensitive to being watched to the point of changing their behavior is evidenced in report after report of anxiety patients' sessions. They fled the classroom, they requested a transfer, they suddenly were unable to speak, they became so confused they were unable to think, they stayed in the bathroom until a caller went home. As in many of the examples cited in preceding chapters, it is typical of my socially phobic patients to feel the weight of another's gaze most acutely and to respond to it dramatically as if to a message of threat.

Many patients, however, are as concerned about the messages they send as with how to respond to others' gazes. Socially phobic people seem to share a belief that there is a "right" and "wrong" way to handle eye behavior and that they have never really gotten the etiquette straight.

Recall the man who wrestled with himself in the hallways at work about appearing either overeager or hostile. A history professor in a small college echoed those same concerns. Although he came to the clinic primarily for help with his public speaking fears, he eventually told me, "I worry about making people uncomfortable. They sense something about me—I don't know exactly what but it has something to do with my eyes. Maybe I glare or stare, I don't know." He reported that he had been told once or twice that he was "scary looking" and did not smile enough. This feedback was enough to rivet his concern on his eye behavior, making his lectures nearly impossible ordeals of self-consciousness and self-doubt.

Many of my male patients have expressed similar concerns

about seeming too intense, strange, wild, or fierce. Whereas socially phobic women seem most concerned that they might unwittingly convey unintended flirtatious or seductive messages, these men seemed to imagine that their gazes could turn into a "whammy" or even a "double whammy" that might inadvertently flash out and zap those who met their eyes. In short, far from worrying about being intimidated and forced to flee by the experience of being watched, these men were concerned about sending out challenges—involunt:. .ly—and provoking retaliation.

BLUSHING

Another source of discomfort associated with the anxiety surrounding eye contact carries the name *erythrophobia*—the fear of blushing.

In many ways, despite the amazing range of messages conveyed by changes around the eyes, our faces are masks that hide our true natures and our private responses to the world. And yet with certain actions, body and psyche conspire to express something of what is going on in that private subjective world. Smiling, laughing, crying, vocalizing in fear or passion or sympathy—all these are involuntary displays of feeling that often escape us despite our resolves to maintain the tightest controls and keep our subjective secrets. Blushing is perhaps the least controllable of all these spontaneous displays, and although it may exist in people who are not socially phobic, it is often present in socially phobic patients (in one study, 51 percent of socially phobic subjects had problems with blushing).[17] I have always considered it a cruel twist of fate when people who already dread and suffer under the scrutiny of others must undergo the added fear or the outright embarrassment of blushing—a betrayal of their deepest, most secret responses to the world they fear spread across their faces for all to see.

Blushing has long been associated with embarrassment, but its relationship with social phobia is more complex than as a simple reaction to a faux pas. Rather, blushing is one component in a vicious cycle that is fueled by another's scrutiny. Once the socially phobic person blushes (or shakes, stammers, or trembles), he or she considers the response a trigger for more harsh judgments—and thus there is no way out. For my patients, their own blushing seems to signal a belief that "the other" has penetrated their privacy and discovered some secret feeling (usually a defect or deficit) that should never have been displayed to the world.

I can often predict who will blush excessively—they almost invariably come to the clinic wearing high collars and long sleeves. Social phobics consider blushing to be a major handicap, especially in their interactions with people of the opposite sex.

Although he was noted for his gregariousness and was not apparently socially phobic, the playwright Tennessee Williams conveyed the agonizing experience of being betrayed by a creeping blush.

> I remember the occasion on which this constant blushing had its beginning. I believe it was in a class in plane geometry. I happened to look across the aisle and a dark and attractive girl was looking directly into my eyes and at once I felt my face burning. It burned more and more intensely after I had faced front again. My God, I thought, am I blushing because she looks into my eyes or I into hers? Suppose this happens whenever my eyes look into the eyes of another? As soon as I had entertained that nightmarish speculation, it was immediately turned into a reality. Literally from that incident on and almost without remission, for the next four or five years, I would blush whenever a pair of human eyes, male or female, would meet mine.[18]

Charles Darwin was also aware of the impediment of blushing; he noted that "it is plain to everyone that young men and women are highly sensitive to the opinion of each other with reference to their personal appearance; and they blush incomparably more in the presence of the opposite sex than on their own." Amazingly, very little work has been done on blushing since 1872, when Darwin pursued the subject. Among his observations are the following:

- Women blush more than men.
- The tendency to blush runs in families.
- People of all races blush.
- The young blush more freely than the old.
- Infants do not appear to blush.

"Most persons while blushing intensely, have their mental powers confused," wrote Darwin. In this condition, people "lose their presence of mind a l utter singularly inappropriate remarks. They are often much distressed, stammer and make awkward movements or strange grimaces. . . . I have been informed by a young lady, who blushed excessively, that at such times she does not even know what she is saying."[19] Clearly, we cannot know whether this young lady was socially phobic, but the description of her responses certainly corresponds with those of patients with high social anxiety.

We do not know exactly what causes blushing. It appears to be vasodilatation, the filling with blood, of the small blood vessels close to the surface of the skin. Darwin noted that, for most people, blushing is limited to the face, neck, and ears. Although this is partially true because the skin tends to be thinner and more visible in these regions, some of my patients report blushing and blotching on their entire bodies. The exact mechanisms responsible for this spread of color are unknown, although some speculate that they have to do with the relaxation of sympathetic tone or, conversely, activation of the parasympathetic component of the autonomic nervous system. Still others speculate that sympathetically aroused beta-adrenocepters may induce vasodilatation.

None of these speculations, however, tell us why blushing occurs. Patients commonly describe a vicious cycle: "First, I become aware of a warmth on my face and then I know I'm blushing. I start to worry about others noticing. My worry seems to add to the intensity of the blushing." In his speculations on the origins and meaning of blushing, Darwin brought to bear his focus on evolution and adaptation. "It is . . . probable," he wrote, "that primitive man before he had acquired much moral sensitiveness would have been highly sensitive about his personal appearance at least in reference to the other sex, and he would, consequently, have felt distressed over any depreciatory remarks about his appearance." However, in the context of social phobia, it is clear that blushing is in no way contingent on negative remarks; one need only be *seen*—or in some cases imagine being seen—to begin to blush. Wrote Darwin, "It is not a simple act of reflecting on our own appearance, but *the thinking of others thinking of us* [my italics] which excites a blush. In absolute solitude, the most sensitive person would be quite indifferent about his appearance—it is notorious that nothing makes a shy person blush so much as any remark, however slighted, on his personal appearance."[20]

I think of Amy in this context, whose blushing was the focus of her extreme anxiety at the party honoring her good work. A partygoer's remark about her beauty caused her to flee the party—and the idea that she might blush while accepting her award had tormented her for months before the actual event.

Darwin and others have speculated rather unsatisfactorily on the possible evolutionary meaning of blushing. Darwin contended that blushing might have once been useful but now "serves no useful function at present." Robert Edelmann, in his book about embarrassment, notes with some irony that blushing occurs "in those moments that generally we wish to hide" and "can hardly help us in our efforts at concealment."[21]

What, then, is the evolutionary function of the blushing response? It is entirely possible that, in the grammar of the nonverbal language, blushing has a specific meaning—and may even have a survival function signaling, for example, an acknowledgment of one's lower status as compared to another, or perhaps even sexual readiness.

However, at this point we have lost the Rosetta Stone that might serve to interpret the physiological signals we, as interactive animals, send to each other at any given moment despite our frustrated and sometimes painful attempts to control them. Perhaps the most significant role that blushing can serve for us now is as a reminder of our biological selves. Like every socially interactive species on earth, as we go through our complex rituals, our minds lost in abstractions, self-consciousness, or fear, our bodies retain their evolutionary memories and speak to each other in a silent language composed of gesture, expression, even sounds and odors beneath our conscious awareness.

"IMAGINED UGLINEᴖS"—BODY DYSMORPHIC DISORDER

It has become a truism to say that we are a society so overly concerned with physical appearance that we are making ourselves sick over it. Nevertheless, as a nation our obsession with our bodies continues to grow. A brief survey of the facts and figures of appearance suggests the scope of the problem.

• Americans spend $33 billion on the diet industry, $20 billion on cosmetics, and $300 billion on plastic surgery annually.
• In 1985, 95 percent of all women believed they weighed too much, while statistics suggest that only about 25 percent (the same as men) were medically overweight.
• A recent study of high school girls found that 53 percent were unhappy with their bodies by the age of thirteen; by the age of eighteen the number dissatisfied was 78 percent.
• In the mid-1980s, 477,000 "esthetic" surgeries had been performed, up 61 percent from 1981.
• In the 1980s, a growing epidemic of eating disorders such as anorexia nervosa and bulimia came to public attention.

Many studies show that physically attractive people have a distinct advantage over less attractive ones. For example, attractive preschoolers are more popular with their peers than unattractive ones; teachers rate attractive children as the smartest and most effective.[22] Tall, lean men earn higher salaries than short, chubby men; and in the accounting business, physical attractiveness was a greater factor in becoming a partner than graduate degrees or quality of schooling. More than one study has shown that attractive defendants seem to receive more positive courtroom judgments than unattractive ones.

When one considers these facts together, the American preoccupation with physical appearance takes on an aspect of mass pathology. And yet hidden among these various aspects of the problem is a level of disturbance regarding the self-perception of one's physical being that is of an entirely different order and that receives very little attention. The clues to this disorder are slight and often subtle, but they indicate an estrangement from the body and a distorted self-image that reflect an underlying mental illness. This condition is called *body dysmorphic disorder*, or *dysmorphophobia*.

One might suppose dysmorphophobia to be a relatively new disorder, perhaps even an outgrowth of our society's overemphasis on physical appearance. In fact, the term was coined more than a hundred years ago by the Italian physician E. Morselli, in 1891. The root word is the Greek dysmorfia, which means ugliness—so dysmorphophobia literally means "fear of one's own ugliness."

It is true that the shy and the very shy are often intensely concerned with their appearance. They worry that they are not "attractive enough," and studies show that they underestimate their own attractiveness as compared to others in assessing their physical appearance.[23] And in some such assessments, it seems, there might be a grain of truth to those self-assessments, since their sometimes awkward, inhibited behaviors are at times rated as unattractive by others.[24] But those with body dysmorphic disorder are not so much concerned with how they measure up as with a sense of "strangeness," or "not-quite-rightness" about their bodies. Such remarks as this, from my case files, might be a red flag suggesting the presence of this disorder: "My eyes are so dull. People think I'm incompetent or stupid because my eyes don't shine." This not as a simple observation but as the expression of a full-blown obsession.

Another man was also deeply troubled by his eyes: "It's the

shape. I can't exactly tell you why they're wrong—they're too big or something. Sometimes I wonder whether they are really my own eyes." On the whole, this patient reported that he was generally quite "cheerful" with regard to his appearance. "But I can't shake the idea that there is something weird about my eyes that somebody might notice. If someone does remark about them, I'm afraid I'll fall apart. Because I don't know myself what the problem is." This man was never in the presence of another person witl ut experiencing intense concern about his eyes.

Some people's apprehensions about their bodies go far beyond the usual insecurities. Raymond, for example, came in at the urging of his wife. A thirty-four-year-old man with many of the symptoms common to socially phobic patients, he reported that he had become so self-conscious over the last few years that he felt that people were staring at him and thinking negative thoughts about him. These concerns had become so great that he was seldom able to leave his house—whereas once he and his wife had had an active social life and he had been an avid golfer, now he resembled an agoraphobic, although his fear was of others' scrutiny, not—as is the root problem in agoraphobia—the fear of panicking.

Further probing revealed that his evaluation anxiety had a single specific source: "It's my legs—they're too skinny. They don't fit the rest of my body. I can see how people react when they look at me—they're shocked. They can hardly believe what I look like. I'm a freak."

Raymond's wife, parents, and minister had repeatedly assured him that his legs looked perfectly normal to them, but he spent many hours in front of a mirror trying to decide on how he should stand or place his legs to give the least offensive view. He embarked on weight training to build up his legs, but was dissatisfied with the results. He never wore shorts and spent days shopping for pants that would fit what he saw as his grotesque lower body. Every so often, at the height of frustration with himself, he made medical appointments—with an internist, orthopedic surgeon, chiropractor—to try to find a solution. As might be imagined, the doctors he consulted were astonished at his desperate insistence that they diagnose and solve his problem.

Dysmorphophobia has been called "the distress of imagined ugliness." It manifests itself as a preoccupation with an imaginary defect or excessive concern over a very slight physical anomaly—perhaps a mole, a bump on the nose, the shape of the eyes, and so on. The disorder is distinguished from anorexia nervosa, another condition that involves a distorted self-perception causing extreme agitation and self-disgust. By contrast, people with anorexia nervosa, a condition characterized by a belief that one is fat and an intense desire to be thin, do not usually appear to feel any particular embarrassment—even when the body has become emaciated and self-consciousness would be appropriate. (Some connections among these conditions, however, need further investigation and explanation. There may be similar causes behind anorexia, bulimia—voluntary purging—and dysmorphia.)

The dysmorphophobe's preoccupation tends to be persistent and leads to marked social dysfunction and, occasionally, behavioral extremes. The disorder has not been well studied, in part because people who experience it tend, if they seek medical attention, to go to surgeons, internists, or dermatologists rather than psychiatrists. (When these specialists refer them to psychiatrists, they feel insulted and dismissed without being taken seriously.) It is estimated that dysmorphophobes constitute 2 percent of plastic surgery patients. Eventually, though, friends or relatives urge such individuals to visit anxiety clinics such as ours, and we are now beginning to realize that the disorder is more common than previously supposed.

Preoccupations can vary from mild to extremely severe and can take many forms; problems often result from a casual remark made by a friend or relative. Common complaints include the shape, size, or other aspect—sometimes a very small or subtle aspect—of the eyes, eyelids, eyebrows, mouth, lips, teeth, jaw, or head. For example, one man grew increasingly agitated because he viewed his nose as disproportionate to his jaw. Another was bothered by a minute scar, so tiny that one could have easily argued that it was imaginary. Some focus on the genitals, breasts, buttocks, hips, shoulders, or skin. One twenty-four-year-old woman came to us after a third cosmetic surgery on her breasts. Originally, she had been concerned that they were "not the right shape." Subsequent surgeries left her only with more dissatisfaction over the shape of her breasts— "they're square-shaped now," she said sadly. She felt that she would be humiliated if anyone learned her secret. She was determined to sue her plastic surgeon, but could find no doctors who could understand what she meant by the "blocky shapes" she was left with.

Not all dysmorphophobic patients have a generalized fear of social situations, but it is common to see patients who have features of body dysmorphic disorder combined with the usual socially phobic symptoms. For example, twenty-five-year-old Alan sought help for the social fears he experienced when he attended classes at a local college. Specifically, he was terrified that he would be called upon in class or would suddenly draw attention in a large lecture hall as he entered. His fears had caused him to begin college and then drop out for four consecutive semesters. He also reported other generalized fears— fears of eating in restaurants, being introduced to strangers (particularly women), and, to some extent, using public restrooms.

A behavior therapist asked Alan to explain his habit of walking with his head down and his gaze lowered. He confided that "I used to believe my penis was too small and would constantly watch the bulge it made while I walked to see if it looked big enough." This concern had dogged him throughout his adolescence and was receding by the time we saw him, but he still admitted that it was hard to resist "an occasional glance." At the root of his fears, as with most dysmorphophobia, was the fear of being judged and humiliated. It is not hard to see why such patients might avoid dating, sexual contact, swimming, shopping, crowds, public events— any of the social contact that can enrich the human condition.

When body dysmorphia and social phobia appear together, they raise questions as to whether the disorders are related. Do people develop social phobic behaviors because of their concerns over appearance? Or, conversely, are people with high social anxiety predisposed to developing specific concerns about appearance? Japanese psychiatrists tend to believe that body dysmorphic disorder is simply a severe form of social phobia, and a small study of five cases found that in dysmorphophobes who were socially phobic, anxiety and social avoidance improved when the body distress improved.[25]

Although social phobia and dysmorphophobia are distinct conditions, we are learning that they sometimes occur along with certain chronic illnesses that involve visible physiological disabilities. For example, Gerry, a forty-year-old accountant, sought help for a performance phobia that was preventing him from pursuing his passion, playing music with a band. He described other fears and behaviors that were consistent with generalized social phobia and described himself as having been shy for as long as he could remember. But his social fears intensified noticeably after he was diagnosed in his late teens as having benign essential tremor, an inherited condition that results in mild shaking of the hands so fine it did not interfere with his playing.

Gerry believed that his tremor disorder may have played a role in his increasing fear of scrutiny. His hands became the focus of his terror of embarrassment, and over time this concern seemed to "spread" to cover other concerns in social situations. He began to fear encounters with more than one person at a time, became unable to play music or write and type when people were watching him, and was unable to eat in restaurants for fear "of making a fool of himself."

In another example, a research group at the National Institutes of Mental Health studied Parkinson's disease, a chronic condition that causes shakiness, stiffness, awkwardness, and other symptoms. Of twenty-four Parkinson patients in this study, 38 percent had anxiety disorders and 4 percent were socially phobic—both rates are significantly higher than might be expected by chance. The investigators speculated about several possible explanations—social phobia in these people might have been a psychological response to their illness, a result of their medications, or the result of an underlying physiological condition causing or contributing to *both* conditions.[26] Other examples might involve people with skin diseases, excessive sweating, severe burn scars, or other disfiguring injuries or illnesses. We are just beginning to look into these confounding situations, and these investigations may shed further light on the causes of social phobia.

A FINAL NOTE

Although social phobia and dysmorphic body disorder share a number of characteristics and in certain circumstances may even be mistaken for each other, there are usually some important differences. Above all, many people with dysmorphophobia tend to have personality features that are classified as schizoid. As a result of these features they tend to prefer a solitary existence, but not because social interaction is a source of anxiety. Typically, in fact, dysmorphophobes do not yearn for social relationships at all, whereas for socially phobic people it is just this yearning, in combination with their anxiety, that is the source of their greatest suffering.

Also, people with body dysmorphia do not consider their anxiety and concern to be inappropriate, and they do not experience the relief that is characteristic for socially phobic people when they are finally alone. Quite the opposite is true—whether alone or with others, people with dysmorphophobia continue to be tortured by what they perceive as their deformities. Socially phobic people, by contrast, often escape the source of their distress only to begin longing for it—and this is perhaps the cruelest irony of the cycle. What many of my patients view as the "key" to a happy life—rich, satisfying, and comfortable interaction—is the very element that eludes them. I wonder whether perhaps the socially phobic, from the safe places to which they withdraw, may not value social interaction even more than the rest of us.

Chapter 8

Trembling in the Wings

Most people are really very frightened. Getting out there on stage is like walking on stage naked—naked and looking awful.
— An actress quoted by Stephen Aaron, in *Stage Fright*

How NATURAL IT SEEMS, and how easy, when great actors take the stage and begin to weave their web of fantasy. The audience waits eagerly to be engulfed in another reality. Through words, inflection, gesture, and tone, that reality quickly builds and takes hold. We empathize with the characters—hope their hopes, dream their dreams, suffer their disappointments, and glory in their victories. Only if their performances fail utterly to capture us do we think about the consciousness *behind* the characters—the subjective experience of the actors and what, behind the art, they are going through.

As most schools of performance acknowledge, that experience can be ghastly indeed. The actor's naturalness and apparent ease on stage are necessary to theater and to the spinning of the web of words that becomes an alternative, temporary reality. But in many cases they mask (the actor hopes) a performance anxiety so extreme that most schools of performing arts and books on acting treat stage fright as a major professional issue.

Contrary to the popular understanding of stage fright, it consists not so much of the fear of flubbing a line or botching an exit as of having one's fright revealed for all in the audience to see. "There is a unique problem of the performing actor," writes Stephen Aaron in *Stage Fright: Its Role in Acting*: "The actor's conscious fear is not that he will make a mistake but that the audience will see something it is not supposed to see, namely, his fear, his stage fright." We can take this explanation one step further by noting that the feared result is not simply being *seen*, and not simply breaking the fantasy of the character, but rather is being seen to be *absurd* by virtue of the fear. In short, stage fright is the intense, nearly debilitating fear of appearing ridiculous. It is clearly a form of social anxiety, and under current classifications, if it is severe enough to interfere with the performer's life, we call it social phobia of a circum-scribed, or discrete, type—that is, social phobia that occurs only in particular situations.

Misconception dogs our understanding of stage fright. The phenomenon is not, as most people imagine, related to inexperience, and it does not go away with practice. Far from it, in fact—many performers experience no decrease of the symptoms even after hundreds of performances, and some become inexplicably afflicted not at the beginning of their careers but suddenly in the middle, or after years of relatively anxiety-free performing. Said the great stage actress Gertrude Lawrence, "These attacks of nerves seem to grow worse with the passing of the years. It's inexplicable and horrible and something you'd think you'd grow out of, not into."[1]

Perhaps the most eloquent description of performance anxiety comes from the greatest actor of our time, Sir Lawrence Olivier. Not until late in his career did this challenge arise, and once it did it plagued him for five years: "My courage sank, and with each succeeding minute it became less possible to resist this horror. My cue came, and I went to the stage where I knew with grim certainty I would not be capable of remaining more than a few minutes. I began to watch for the instant at which my knowledge of my next line would vanish. Only the next two now, now—one more . . . and then *now* I took one pace forward and stopped abruptly. My voice had started to fade, my throat closed up and the audience began to go giddily round (why is it always anti-clockwise?). . . . Unhappily this malaise had a most obstinate reluctance to come to a conclusion. It persisted and continued to torment me for five whole years." So intense did Olivier's fear become that during a performance of *Othello*, he begged the actor playing Iago not to leave the stage, despite an exit called for by the stage directions, "since I feared I might not be able to stay there in front of the audience by myself."[2] Throughout Olivier's description of his agony, it is clear that even more horrible than the inexplicable fear itself is the terrible possibility that the fear will break through the mask and become humiliatingly visible to all.

Though Olivier's explanation conveys the essence of performance anxiety in minute detail, Rosalind Russell's well-known description of acting captures its essence in a single stroke: "Acting," she said, "is standing up naked and turning around very slowly."[3] Unexpressed but all too clearly implied is the potential for humiliation in being fully revealed—that is, naked and unmasked—and scrutinized.

Anecdotes involving performers in many branches of show business abound, differing only in the way the condition expresses itself, not the condition itself. Consider, for example, the actress who vomits before going on stage. According to Aaron, "buckets have to be placed by each of her entrance positions." Far from overcoming her stage fright by growing more familiar with the material, she has had to accept the condition as permanent and figure out ways to live with it and still perform.[4]

Not only its intensity but also this stubborn intransigence distinguishes stage fright from the normal anxiety most people feel before and at the inception of some sort of a performance. And this quality too alerts us to the fact that the condition is a form of social phobia—in this case, a discrete social phobia consistently linked to the performance situation. Remember, for a diagnosis of social phobia to be made, the problematic behavior must interfere with one's normal routine. It seems fair to call the need to vomit into a bucket just before each stage entrance an interference with the normal performance behavior.

CAREERS AT RISK

Performers' livelihoods depend on their public appearances, and the permanence of performance anxiety can literally destroy a career, if not destroy their love of the performing art itself. The great pianist Vladimir Horowitz quit performing entirely for a period of fifteen years and was nearly incapacitated by anxiety when he did manage to perform. Artur Rubenstein, Pablo Casals, and Luciano Pavarotti are all musicians who have reported extreme anxious distress around performance. Casals, perhaps the most renowned cellist of our time, stated, "Nerves and stage fright before playing have never left me throughout the whole of my career."[5]

With their careers and substantial incomes at stake, performers often do prolonged battle with stage fright in the vain effort to overcome it. Contemporary songwriter and singer Carly Simon, for example, battled a lifelong problem with severe stage fright that greatly restricted her ability to sing in public. In 1981, shortly after releasing a million-selling record, Simon made an effort to conquer her fright by embarking on a tour of large concert halls. "After two songs, I was still having palpitations. . . . I fell to pieces on stage in front of everybody. . . . I collapsed before the second show with 10,000 people waiting. . . . The larger the audience, the more I feel I have got to lose."[6] A six-year absence from the stage followed. Whether Simon's perception of "falling apart" was accurate or, as is more likely, an interpretation of events colored by her extreme anxiety, the costs of the disorder and the near impossibility of self-cure are poignantly dramatized by her struggle.

Barbra Streisand also has publicly shared her struggles with performance anxiety related to singing. According to reports in the popular press, she is able to perform at charity functions, like the Clinton Inaugural gala, but has been unable to perform as a paid performer for twenty-seven years.[7]

Recalling Ned, my dentist patient who rated his own audience, his patients, by degree of threat based on their insurance status, is it possible that Miss Streisand believes a paying audience may be more critical or judgmental? The factors that heighten the potential risk of a situation may be highly individualized.

This form of career sabotage from within is by no means limited to stage performers. From time to time, well-known, highly paid sports figures, particularly baseball players, find themselves unable to make the correct plays but make, instead, incomprehensible moves for all the world to see. Upon close examination, these apparently inexplicable personal peculiarities turn out to result from social phobias—in effect, these individuals are forced by their anxious fear of behaving bizarrely in public into actually doing so. Consider, for example, Los Angeles Dodger second baseman Steve Sax, whose performance anxiety expressed itself as an inability to make routine throws to first base; Mike Ivie, a highly promising young catcher for the San Diego Padres, who became so phobic about throwing the ball back to the pitcher that he had to give up his position; and Steve Blass, Pittsburgh Pirate World Series hero and All-Star pitcher, who suddenly, mysteriously, in 1973 could not get the ball over the plate—in a game.[8] Blass continued to throw with near perfection in practice, but in facing hitters lost all control. His anxiety put an end to his career at the age of thirty-two. New York Met catcher Mackey Sasser had to devise a method of returning the ball to the mound so strange that his fear of making a fool of himself threatened to become a realized prophecy with every throw. "To return the ball," wrote a *New York Times Magazine* journalist, "Sasser goes through a bizarre routine of double-pumping, leaning back as if he might fall over and launching return tosses that arch to the mound like basketball free throws. That arch has allowed base runners ... to steal bases." Despite Sasser's terrific talent—"in today's market, left-handed catchers who bat .300 and throw out base stealers (he has no problem throwing to second base) command $2 million a year"—his inability to return the ball cost him his job. Though Sasser's case drew perhaps the most attention to the condition, which afflicted him only when people were watching and never in an empty stadium, a long line of sufferers in the game preceded him, prompting sports psychiatrist Allan Lans to term the syndrome "disreturnaphobia."[9]

Lans's view of the condition as limited to baseball is misleading, since it obscures its real nature as a form of social phobia. Still, "disreturnaphobia" *is* significant, because it demonstrates that speaking and fine motor skills, such as writing, are not the only kinds of behavior disrupted by social phobia. In these examples drawn from baseball, we have evidence that gross motor skills such as throwing a ball are vulnerable as well. Just as a social phobic may be unable to sign a check in public due to the fear of revealing a trembling hand, so a star catcher may be unable to return a baseball to the pitcher.

PERFORMING IN EVERYDAY LIFE

I opened this chapter on performance anxiety with dramatic examples of celebrities. But one need not be rich and famous to have severe performance anxiety. In fact, quite the opposite is the case. Whether all of us like it or not, performing has become a fact of contemporary life. At no time in history has it been more necessary for us to pull away from the pack in some way and draw attention to ourselves in public. Perhaps to some extent this phenomenon has to do with the pop-sociology notion that "unless it's on TV it didn't really happen." Thus, even in walks of life once known for their isolation—writing, for example, or research science—committed individuals desiring to progress feel the pressure to "go public."

So, as never before, business people are making presentations, book writers are "going out on tour," artists are entering public forums, ordinary citizens are going on talk shows to air their problems. People who may have chosen their particular pursuits out of a love of their work or other personal motivations frequently find themselves in the position of talking to groups of strangers as a requirement for continuing. In this regard, the writer, actor, and director Andre Gregory once recounted how a well-known Buddhist Roshi had told him that the three great fears of the Japanese are dying, going insane, and public speaking. "What in God's name do these three things have in common?" Gregory asked him. "Think about it," the Roshi replied. "Each one involves entering the unknown."[10]

To many who never dreamed that they would be public figures, all the world has indeed become a stage, and a huge percentage of our total population dreads stepping up in front of an audience beyond just about everything else. For example, survey results show that from 30 to 43 percent of the total U.S. population names public speaking their number one fear—ahead of heights, sickness, death, loneliness, and the dark. And 25 percent of Americans who name another fear as number one report having "much fear" of speaking before groups.

Given this level of apprehension, it is not surprising that many worry anxiously about these moments as they are approaching, avoid them whenever possible, and endure them if they have to with extreme discomfort. The crisis of an appearance before a group is often the "straw" that breaks an individual's resolve to cope themselves with psychological distress and to seek help. At this point, whatever tactics a person might have been using to "get through" have failed, or the person fears that they will fail, and he or she becomes immobilized by fear.

It is interesting to note that many people who fear public performance are quite comfortable in social situations—again, these people are diagnosed as suffering from a discrete, localized performance anxiety as opposed to generalized social phobia, which renders the sufferer terrified in most situations involving other people.

In actual practice, however, close examination in the cases of many patients and professional performers reveals that what initially appeared to be a discrete performance anxiety was only the tip of the iceberg, the most prominent and disabling portion of a series of fears that interfere with many other aspects of their lives. One study of British orchestral musicians, for example, found that those with stage fright commonly experienced other social fears related to appearing in crowds and other social situations.[11]

SOCIAL PHOBIA AS OCCUPATIONAL HAZARD

What distinguishes an accomplished performance from an amateur one is its seeming effortlessness. Think about a virtuoso performance by such a master as Jascha Heifitz, for example. Part of the pleasure, from the point of view of the audience, is wonderment at the apparent ease with which the maestro makes the musical offering. And yet it was the great violinist Heifitz who once remarked, in reference to his struggles with performance anxiety, that his audience came to his performances only to witness his mistakes.

In fact, performance anxiety—under an array of names including stage fright, public speaking anxiety, and audience anxiety—is not a freak occurrence but an all-too-familiar complaint among performing professionals of all types. For example, in a study of students and faculty at the University of Iowa School of Music, 16.5 percent of the subjects indicated that their musical performances were impaired by the anxiety of performing; 21 percent indicated that they experienced "marked distress" while performing; and 16.1 percent indicated that their performance anxiety had adversely affected their careers.[12]

In a major survey conducted by the International Conference of Symphony and Opera Musicians, 24 percent of the 2,212 professional classical musicians questioned reported an ongoing problem with performance anxiety.[13] Other studies have shown an increase of drug and alcohol abuse among performers. Many performers report self-medicating with a sedative or alcohol as a way of getting through a performance. Sir Lawrence Olivier, after five years of fearing that his stage fright "would mean a mystifying and scandalously sudden retirement," finally confided his problem to his friends in the theater, Sir Lewis Casson and his wife, actress Dame Sybil Thorndike. In a famed reply that undoubtedly cheered Olivier enormously, Dame Sybil told him, "Take drugs, darling. We do."[14]

Music, theater, even law schools, have long recognized the problem of performance anxiety as an inherent occupational hazard. Until recently, though, when the phenomenon came under serious study as a defined psychological condition, these institutions did their best to address these problems in such workshops or conferences as "Coping with Performance Anxiety," "Techniques for Management of Stage Fright," and "Understanding and Preventing Performance Stress." No doubt attendees gained some relief simply from learning that they were not alone in their distress, even if the techniques they learned for controlling their anxiety were based more on intuition than firm evidence. And yet research has convinced us that practice alone is simply not enough to cure performance anxiety.

SIGNS AND SYMPTOMS

What happens to people with performance anxiety when they expose themselves to the scrutiny of others by speaking, acting, singing, playing an instrument, or even playing competitive sports? An array of studies demonstrate extreme physiological changes in anticipation of and/or during the course of a performance. Findings include accelerated heartbeat, cardiac abnormalities such as skipped heartbeats or palpitations, a rise in the levels of neurotransmitters such as epinephrine (adrenalin) or norepinephrine in the blood, and increases in blood pressure. One even occasionally hears of speakers collapsing and even dying of cardiovascular incidents in the midst of a presentation.[15] All these data suggest high levels of activation of the sympathetic branch of the autonomic nervous system and the adrenal glands. In our research at the University of Wisconsin, we found that during the planning stage prior to a feared speech, people with social phobia showed high activation of their right cerebral hemispheres, reflecting the extreme intensity of their apprehension. This activation appeared to interfere both with the logical and verbal preparation for the speaking task.

These dramatic bodily changes are commonly accompanied by some or all of the following cardiovascular symptoms: an uncomfortable awareness of an increased heart rate; blushing; a feeling of light-headedness accompanied by a fear of fainting; tremor or shakiness; weakness in the legs; nausea and a feeling of being close to vomiting; and occasionally a sense of urinary or bowel urgency.

In addition, people with performance anxiety often suffer symptoms related to their specific art. For example, speakers, actors, and singers might have to contend with an extremely dry mouth or a constriction of the throat. One British actor had to arrange to be dressed and made up by an assistant, because anxiety made him "so out of control that he is unable to perform these functions for himself. . . . Left to his own devices, he often forgets what play he's in and will sometimes appear costumed for another piece in the repertory." The symptoms of performance anxiety can sometimes take the form of what seems to be a terrible joke custom-designed to humiliate the dedicated performer. Aaron quotes Maureen Stapleton to demonstrate the intensity and variety of the symptoms: "When I work, it starts about six-thirty at night. I start to burp. I belch—almost nonstop. I keep burping, all through the show, right up to the curtain, and right after, and then I'm all right."[16] What could be worse for one frightened to death at the prospect of public humiliation than the threat of an on-stage siege of uncontrollable gastric gas?

In addition to the physiological symptoms that build toward a dreaded performance, many of my patients experience a storm of uncontrollable thoughts: "I'm going to faint [or vomit, or blush, or shake]," "A mistake is just moments away—it's inevitable," or "They'll all see how inadequate I am—they'll know I'm a fraud." Often these thoughts coalesce into an overall sentence of doom: "I'm just about to humiliate myself hopelessly—I'll lose my job, it will ruin my life, and there's nothing that can avert the catastrophe."

It is possible for all these psychological and physiological symptoms to coalesce into a nearly unbearable crescendo of feelings and behaviors during the feared performance itself— almost as if they were designed to wreck the performance and fulfill the prophecy of imagined humiliation. One of my patients, for example, had to give a slide show to a group of peers in his company. Already in a state of high anxiety, during the presentation he realized that several of his slides were out of order. He had to stop and endure the silence and gazes at his back while he frantically sorted through the slides. This plus the agitation of presenting in public at all—the perspiration, racing heart palpitations, and shaking hands—overwhelmed him. With no explanation, he suddenly left the projector running and departed.

This survey of the symptoms and manifestations of performance anxiety should sound familiar by now. Although rarely perceived as such in the theater, performance anxiety is a form of social anxiety and, at its most extreme, social phobia.

ANTICIPATORY ANXIETY

Like other forms of social anxiety, performance anxiety encompasses not only the actual performance but the anticipation of the upcoming ordeal as well. "There is ample evidence," writes Paul Salmon, in an article reviewing performance anxiety among musicians, "that many anxious thoughts have a future orientation, with a focus on things that may, but not necessarily will, happen. Anxious musicians worry incessantly about upcoming performances and any number of catastrophes that may befall them."[17]

In fact, there is some evidence that experienced performers reach a peak of fear just prior to the performance, whereas novices reach their peaks during the performance. And some data suggest that for the experienced performer anticipatory anxiety can actually *benefit* the performance, because it provides an opportunity to practice coping with the feared events.

THEORIES

What accounts for extreme performance anxiety? Why do some people have it while others do not? Various theories have emerged to answer these questions. One proposes relatively simple reasons for the phobia, such as poor preparation or faulty skills. Another suggests that actual failure in the past triggers fear of a repeat of the painful experience in the future—thus, the person "learns" to be anxious in response to a stimulus. But most people who suffer performance anxiety are unable to point to specific failures that they feel initiated their anxiety responses. In fact, many of my clients are very clear about having made excellent, well-received, all-around successful performances in the past.

A similar but more subtle theory suggests that the normal physiological responses to any public performance—rapid heartbeat, palpitations, sweating, and shakiness—come to be *associated* with and then experienced as fear even after the person has grown accustomed to the performance situation. In other words, *all* people experience these responses when they perform, but only social phobics come to interpret the responses as fear.

In this view, the normal responses, triggered by the autonomic nervous system, may initiate a vicious cycle. Here's an example:

- On the morning of a presentation at the regional corporate conference, Jack begins to anticipate the experience of facing an audience of 200.
- As the hour approaches and he imagines the scene in detail, Jack becomes aware that his heart is pounding, his palms are sweating, and his limbs are shaking.
- He interprets these responses as signals that he is, in his own words, "absolutely petrified of making an ass of myself."
- In fact, the very existence of the responses—or, in Jack's case as a socially phobic individual, symptoms—gives him cause to believe he *will* humiliate himself. After all, what could be more humiliating than revealing to the whole company that one is a nervous wreck, especially in a culture that sets public composure as one of its highest values?

ANXIETY VERSUS AROUSAL

The theory I have just elaborated is attractive, because it incorporates several ideas familiar in human psychology. One such idea is that what one person calls anxiety is another's beneficial arousal. We know that a state of heightened arousal—which is characterized by many of the same autonomic responses under discussion—can be helpful to many kinds of performances. In fact, many athletes, musicians, and other kinds of performers report that their absence leaves them with a feeling of "flatness" and the inability to perform at their best. Many team athletes in the postgame explanation say things like "we just didn't get up for it," "you could tell in the locker room that nobody was excited," "we were too casual," or "we just weren't turned on, we weren't at our peak."

The second familiar idea is that some individuals are hypervigilant when it comes to their own internal cues. While others are able to ignore their autonomic symptoms of psychological arousal, stage fright sufferers, as well as other socially phobic people, may be so "tuned in" to changes within that they are unable to "tune out" the bodily changes that accompany performance or other forms of social interaction. In the same way, hypochondriacs may be more sensitive to their internal bodily sensations than nonhypochondriacs. The reasons for such a hypersensitivity may well be genetic—many socially phobic people, to the question of when their troubles started, answer that they have "always been that way."

The fact that a particular drug treatment for social phobia involving beta blockers has had some success gives weight to the theory that social phobia involves the *subjective interpretation* of the symptoms rather than the symptoms themselves. This class of medicines, used primarily to treat high blood pressure and heart disease, blocks the beta-adrenergic receptors of the autonomic nervous system. When these receptors are stimulated by such neurotransmittors as adrenalin, they respond by triggering the very responses listed as symptoms by the performer—shakiness, palpitations, increased heart rate, and so on. By blocking the production of these symptoms, the drug interrupts the vicious cycle.

As I will discuss more fully in chapter 10, on treatment, substantial "underground" traffic in beta blockers among performers testifies to the fact that these drugs indeed take the painful edge off the experience of performing. As a matter of fact, a series of double-blind studies actually suggests that the drugs *improve* performance from the standpoint of the observer, especially when the activity involves fine hand or finger movements.

Nevertheless, attractive as it is, this theory—sometimes referred to as the "somatic symptom feedback model"—is insufficient to explain performance anxiety entirely. Several kinds of evidence suggest that performance anxiety is more than a simple response to one's own bodily sensations: most patients who have been treated with beta blockers continue to experience some anxiety. Thus, patients might report, "Sure, my heart wasn't pounding the way it would without the drug, but that didn't mean I wasn't scared."

We also know that patients with severe spinal cord injury who do not have autonomic nervous system activity nevertheless feel anxiety. And, finally, people with very high heart rates, high blood pressure, excessive sweating, and other autonomic arousal responses do not necessarily rate themselves as more anxious than others, with lower levels of these responses.

So, again, one person's anxiety may be another's arousal. The key seems to be that although subjective experiences and one's interpretation of body clues are important contributors to the experience of performance anxiety, there is a significant central nervous system component as well, one that feeds and intensifies one's fear in the performing situation.

BAD-MOUTHING ONESELF

The stubborn tenacity of performance anxiety is one of its greatest puzzles. "Habituation"—the gradual, incremental exposure to the feared situation under professional guidance—has long been a cornerstone of treatment for phobias of other kinds, but as I have suggested, professional performers may not "get used to" the performing situation despite repeatedly forcing themselves through it. It is speculation at this point, but this fact alone makes us wonder whether perhaps people with severe performance anxiety and/or general social phobia habituate differently from normal people.

The failure of habituation to work has made us seek other explanations for the tenacity of performance anxiety. Of central significance may be the level of negative thoughts about the self experienced by people with performance anxiety. Research shows that people with high levels of performance anxiety are much more likely than others to experience catastrophic thinking—for example, "something terrible is going to happen to me if I go before this group." In these self-perpetuating thoughts, specific themes tend to emerge:

- Inadequacy. "As soon as I open my mouth and they hear my voice shake, they'll realize right away that I'm a fraud."
- Anticipation of punishment. "Somebody in the group will tell my boss how scared I looked and I'll lose my job."
- Criticism. "I'm just setting myself up by talking in public. Everything I've been doing for the past two years is going to be up for grabs and they'll see how weak my thinking really is."
- Loss of stature. "I can just picture the other dancers in my class They're like vultures. The minute I start they're going to be giggling hysterically together. There's no way I'll ever advance to the next level, no way I can ever be a professional dancer. This recital will finish my dreams for a career forever."

People with a steady stream of negative thoughts are also more likely than more optimistic performers to interpret their bodily sensations as evidence of potential disaster. So, even though the person may experience relatively mild autonomic responses, the anticipation of disaster might be maintained by the internal self-talk preventing habituation from taking place.

WHY ANXIETY?

Though all these mechanisms are of interest, they still do not explain *why* performing produces so much anxiety in the first place—and not just in certain people but, initially at least, in just about everybody. The answer to the why of performance anxiety may not be so mysterious if viewed from an evolutionary perspective. At one level, of course, we know that being viewed, looked at, watched, stared at, or scrutinized activates arousal responses in everyone. Surely, placing oneself in a performance situation in front of an audience is the ultimate portrayal of this stress, whether the viewing is actual as in live performances, or more symbolic, as with recordings, radio, television, or movies. Perhaps Frederick Elworthy, a nineteenth-century English actor, was on to something when he speculated that Greek actors in the ancient theaters wore masks not to represent their characters but to "protect themselves from the evil eye of the spectator."[18]

However, performing may arouse less conscious and more primitive feelings in front of one's peers or worse, one's superiors. At a subconscious level, the performance situation probably activates primitive dominant/submissive concerns. In this context, performance is viewed as an open display of the performer's strength, skill, prowess, perhaps even self-worth—in short, it exhibits one's resource-holding potential. At some level it is a bid for increased status (or at the very least, maintenance of present status) or a challenge to one's peers or superiors. A semiawareness of this function of self-display and its consequent risks makes the performance frightening. Specifically, such open display could call forth criticism or negative judgments that might result in the loss of status in one's peer group, and accompanying loss of self-esteem, and—the very worst—ostracism. These days, fortunately, the person trembling in the wings may tremble only in a symbolic sense at the prospect of banishment from the safety and security that group living affords. Therefore, although loneliness and sudden death may not often be consequences of performance failure, many of my patients respond as if they were. It is possible that stepping up in front of a group epitomizes the situation of being evaluated by one's group, and the individual fears that his or her peers are searching for clues as to where or even *if* the individual in question fits into the social hierarchy.

Unlike a person involved in a social interaction, a performer is also handicapped by the lack of immediate feedback. He or she must wait to see the response to the performance and, thus, is left to imagine, for better or worse, how he or she is being perceived and judged. This vacuum is an opportunity for distress to build.

In this same vein, because of the lack of the opportunity to interact, performers who feel that they are failing in their dominance display, are overmatched, or are being appraised critically, are unable to convey the usual social signals of submission—they cannot say they are sorry, make fun of themselves, or self-depreciate during the "show." Only the more primitive responses remain, such as fainting, fleeing, or being immobilized, precisely those that a person struck with stage fright fears the most. In our clinic, not just entertainers but teachers, executives, and many others whose work requires some degree of public speaking have come in for treatment with performance anxiety so intense that it threatened their ability to do their work.

Chapter 9

Self-Medication with Alcohol and Drugs

Wine drunk with an equal quantity of water puts away anxiety and terrors.
—Hippocrates

B RIAN HAD BEEN PICKED UP for drunk driving four times, and the court remanded him to an inpatient alcoholic treatment program followed by outpatient therapy with a heavy emphasis on group therapy. Brian went through the detoxification portion of the program with little or no resistance. He attended one group session in the residential program, but throughout he remained absolutely mute and rigid.

A big, physically intimidating man of thirty-four, from the outside Brian seemed withdrawn, belligerent, and angry. Later, though, he told me that he had been sleepless for two nights before the session and was in terror during it lest the psychologist focus on him and allow the others to fall silent and watch. "I'm not sitting there blabbing to a bunch of strangers. God, I didn't know what to do," he said. "I knew they'd see what a wimp I was no matter what—if I tried to speak, if I couldn't speak. . . . My heart was beating so hard I thought I'd pass out right in front of them. Like a goddam girl."

After several attempts to involve Brian in the group process, the psychologist allowed Brian to stay in his shell. However, the directors of the program were adamant: participate fully in the groups or go home. This was an expensive, effective, carefully orchestrated program, and there were to be no deviations from the step-by-step approach that had helped a great many patients wean themselves from substance abuse.

Brian dropped out of the program—and his parents, to their great unhappiness, forfeited the sizable treatment fee. Understandably, they were not only disappointed but angry, and afraid that Brian's old patterns of solitary drinking and drug use would soon take hold again. "He just loves to be high more than anything," his father told me. "There's *nothing* that's going to make him give that stuff up."

Brian's father was wrong. Brian heard me on the radio describing social phobia and realized instantly that he was more than just "grumpy and unsociable," as family mythology had it; the description of the disorder applied to him. He took down the number of the clinic and then promptly began to visualize— to the point of near paralysis—coming to the clinic and discussing his problem. Still, with a dawning relief at the possibility that his problems might actually have a name, he realized that no one, including himself, had ever thought of his problems from this perspective. Finally, he called to make an appointment for treatment.

I treated Brian with a benzodiazepine, a class of medications that is controversial among drug and alcohol treatment specialists. He responded well and, after my explanation of the anxiety disorder underlying his drinking, the court accepted our anxiety clinic program in place of the previously mandated one. We will return to Brian's story in chapter 10, when I take a detailed look at benzodiazepines and the controversy they have engendered.

NUMBERS TELL THE STORY

The psychiatric literature documents a very significant correla-
tion between the abuse of alcohol and all the anxiety disorders,
but particularly social phobia. And it is not uncommon for new
patients to confide—usually after a number of sessions—that
they needed a drink, or more, before each of our office visits.
One patient who was being switched to a new medication called
to ask, "Would it be okay with you if I had several drinks before
our session? I don't think I can talk with you now that we've
stopped my medicine."

"You sound all right to me now," I remarked.

"Right. I'm stoned out of my mind. I've been working up to
this since yesterday, and I wrote down what I wanted to say and
rehearsed for an hour before I called you."

Social phobics, more than patients with any other anxiety
disorder, say that they use alcohol and certain drugs to relieve
anxiety. Marijuana tends to discourage social interaction and
psychedelics tend to confuse it, so when the goal is to get
through unavoidable contact, the drugs most favored in this
regard are those with sedative or inhibitory effects—such as barbiturates, meprobamate, and other prescription "downers" used
as street drugs.

Virtually no research has been conducted on the relationship between anxiety disorders and other addictive drugs such as
cocaine and heroin, but patient self-reports regarding alcohol
use correspond with published reviews of the research literature.
These reviews demonstrate that in populations of patients in
treatment for alcohol problems, as many as 68.7 percent have
anxiety problems as well. And several studies have found specifically that as many as 50 percent of inpatients in treatment for
alcoholism were socially phobic.[1]

The converse is also true: studies of social phobics find a
high rate of alcohol use and abuse. The range of figures is relatively widespread, but one study showed that 50 percent of diagnosed social phobics resorted to alcohol use before attending a
social event.[2] Another project reported that 20 percent of the

socially phobic men and 13 percent of the women studied had a lifetime diagnosis of alcoholism. This study also found that the social phobics who were alcoholic were more severely afflicted with social phobia than nonalcoholic social phobics. A further indication that their phobias were more severe was that these dual sufferers were less likely than nonalcoholic social phobics to be married.[3]

THE URGE TO SELF-MEDICATE

The tendency of many socially phobic people to seek relief through drugs and alcohol should come as no surprise. Drinking to relax inhibitions is a norm in our society, one that is expressed in the tradition of the cocktail party. At the end of the week we invite friends and acquaintances to join us at home or a restaurant or a bar, where we make sure there is enough alcohol to "loosen everybody up." With the full social support of the culture as a whole, we lift our glasses and toast each other, tacitly agreeing that we deserve this chemical aid in "winding down" after a difficult week. It does not take a social scientist to recognize the changes in people's comfort level, the conversation pace and volume, the frequency of smiles and laughter, and diminishing physical distance between party guests. And not only do people stand closer together and discuss more personal matters as the liquid lubricant does its work, but they touch each other more often and speak without embarrassment—or perhaps with embarrassment delayed until the next day.

"Often by the time I went to a bar or party," one woman told me, "I'd be completely loaded. I tried to conceal the fact that I'd been drinking ahead of time, but gradually my boyfriends accused me of being a drunk. The thing is, I couldn't be with them at all if I wasn't well on my way to be plastered, so there was no way out." This woman, in her early forties when I met her, saw loneliness as her enemy. She had had a long string of sexually passionate relationships that had gone nowhere. Not until she understood her diagnosis as a social phobic did she recognize the pattern: she would meet a man, drink to be with him, and then any attempt to remain sober would threaten to turn the relationship into a shambles ("Whenever I tried they always asked me, What *is* it? What's the *matter?* You're not yourself!"), so she'd drink until they accused her of being an alcoholic, and that would be the end. It was at this point, after many years of psychoanalysis in the attempt to understand what it was that caused her to drink so s. -destructively, that she recognized the drinking as a response to an underlying problem, profound social anxiety.

THE ALCOHOL/ANXIETY CONNECTION

The fact is, for many socially anxious people, self-medicating does work—fleetingly. Alcohol and some recreational street drugs function to stimulate the release of neurotransmitters in the brain— chemical triggers that facilitate the firing of brain cells that perform specific functions. The result of this receptor stimulation, according to current theory, is the activation of neurotransmitters that inhibit anxiety. Subjectively, the result of this biochemical process is social ease, experienced as pleasure, that seduces the users of chemical intoxicants to continue to use despite the side effects: slurred speech, slowed thoughts, memory failure, poor motor control, and the possibility of addiction. Interestingly, the prescription drugs used to treat social phobia appear to affect the same neurons in the same ways. If used improperly in the absence of medical supervision, these drugs have the identical side effects—side effects that are not only socially debilitating but also potentially dangerous.

More than one of my patients with little experience in social drinking have drunk themselves into a stupor—in the effort to calm themselves before or during a social situation, only to add to the very humiliation in the eyes of others that they feared so intensely. But even when drinking clearly eases the anxiety and allows the social phobic to function, there is the possibility that drug and alcohol use itself may actually interfere with some natural desensitization of social fears that most people experience as social situations are repeated. Thus, while drinking may *temporarily* calm anxiety, in the long run it may actually interrupt the natural psychological processes designed to alleviate it for good.

It is also possible that alcohol interferes with the cognitive process that results in extreme or exaggerated self-awareness. One writer quoted an alcoholic who attempted to identify the cause of his drinking. "Everyone I met in Alcoholics Anonymous was pathologically shy. When I think of why, I am struck by the reason for my own alcoholism being that *drinking turns off the ever-present monitor.* Overdrinking turns it too far off into social irresponsibility, but I suspect that alcoholics do drink to begin with because they are shy."[4]

I need not belabor the point that alcoholism and drug use are two social problems that have brought our society to the point of crisis. Our familiarity with this issue is good news, since not too long ago alcohol and drug use were viewed by many as exciting and positive contributions to the American way of life. But the negative side is that as a society our view of these difficulties remains so muddled we hardly know how to think about them in order to take remedial action. It behooves us all, users and caregivers alike, to reflect further on just what lies below the surface to explain our spiraling addictions. The central connection between chemical abuse and social anxiety urgently demands attention.

From the users' point of view, consider the situation in which drugs or alcohol have been used for so long and so consistently to self-medicate against social phobia that the user rarely notices the root cause, and therefore never even considers seeking treatment for it. In another common scenario, patients and caregivers alike tend to identify intense social anxiety with the withdrawal anxiety that accompanies temporary cessation of an addictive substance, and thus they focus on the latter while the real cause remains unaddressed.

If these circumstances conspire to make the diagnosis of a drug- or alcohol-using social phobic difficult—that is, if the person even finds the way into treatment—a more hidden, perhaps even more stubborn problem compounds the issue: a widespread reluctance on the part of clinical psychologists and psychiatrists to treat alcoholics and drug users. Not only are they untrained in addiction treatment, but in many cases they are temperamentally unsuited for it. Members of my profession tend to downplay the psychologi. l significance of such symptoms and/or avoid such patients, sending them off to alcohol- and drug-treatment programs with the words, "You need to get your drinking, or your drug problem, under control before I can treat you." One result is extremely sketchy "history taking" regarding the interaction of psychiatric or psychological symptoms and chemical abuse. For all these reasons, any possibility of putting the horse in front of the cart—identifying social phobia as a possible *cause* of the addiction—is lost.

TAKING ANOTHER LOOK

Many socially phobic patients with drug or alcohol problems begin to abuse these substances early in life. In a study of 1,300 high school students, for example, Randy Page, a public health researcher, found striking evidence that shyness played a role in adolescent drug and alcohol use. And of the teenagers studied, supershy male adolescents were more likely than shy or nonshy adolescents to use chemical intoxicants—including alcohol, hallucinogenic substances, cocaine, and marijuana. Page hypothesized that "traditional male roles may require initiative in social contacts to a much greater degree than the more passive feminine stereotype and, as a result, the burden of shyness may be especially severe for adolescent boys."[5] As old sex roles continue to break down and new social rituals emerge, we can expect to see this burden shared by females.

This same study of high school students found that very shy

boys appear to gravitate socially to groups in which substance use is more likely to occur. Do these groups provide a more comfortable, less inhibiting social atmosphere? Are obviously shy people more easily pressured into drug use and thus, for their drug-using peers, "easy marks"? It was further postulated that the very shy girls were less likely to place themselves in situations involving underage drinking. Will increased assertiveness among adolescent girls become a marker for increased drug use—that is, with the erosion of the passive female stereotype, will the male/female discrepancy in drug and alcohol use even out?

It is imperative that chemical abuse programs attempting to respond to and treat teenagers be aware of the relationship between social discomfort and the urge to "self-medicate" for social anxiety and social phobia. Some writers who study adolescent alcoholism have postulated that loneliness is a primary cause of chemical abuse. Such a suggestion matches the fundamental belief woven into the Alcoholics Anonymous approach that loneliness precipitates drinking. This suggestion is particularly interesting in our context, since one possible factor that results in loneliness—social anxiety that leads to the avoidance of social contact—is also one that precedes full-blown social phobia. Page, who directed the study cited earlier, suggests that drug-intervention efforts for adolescents should emphasize social skills training and confidence building.[6] This is a solid, psychologically sound suggestion, since adolescence is a critical phase in the development of interpersonal comfort.

Moreover, given adolescents' extreme susceptibility to peer pressure, I would strongly urge that any program designed to treat chemical abuse in teenagers or to head off such problems before they take hold strenuously emphasize "refusal skills." Even socially adept adolescents have difficulty holding out against the pressure of their peers to partake of drink and drugs. Consider the difficulty, then, of a teenager with extreme shyness who is heading down the path toward social phobia. A practical, easy-to-implement solution would be to develop as many word-for-word formulas as we can as ways to respond to social pressures to conform around drugs and alcohol. Verbally skilled and comfortable teenagers might well be able to come up with their own refusals, but socially phobic youngsters might respond with "okay" only because they are too agitated with anxiety to come up with anything else. For them, word-for-word formulas, maybe even in written form to enable practice, could ultimately be a lifesaver. This is, of course, not a cure for social anxiety, but it is a coping tool.

One of my patients who .. not an alcoholic threw the alcohol/anxiety relationship into a clear perspective. Alan, a classic sociophobe, was constantly worried about his eyes ("They're too big, especially when I'm talking to somebody. I can feel them opening up and I become completely distracted, trying to keep them normal"), and as are many young men, he was also concerned about the size of his penis. It was Alan who, as described earlier, could not keep himself from staring down at his crotch to see whether there was a "large enough" bulge.

Alan did not drink regularly and had no history of drug use. In fact, to Alan the notions of drugs and alcohol conjured up terrifying pictures of wild social scenes with everyone laughing and acting crazy except himself. He was afraid that adding these unpredictable substances to the mix would increase his anxiety rather than reduce it, and so he avoided opportunities to experiment. Once, however, at a family wedding that he was unable to avoid, he was afraid he would draw attention to himself by refusing champagne to toast the wedding couple, so he drank two glasses and then slipped away from the reception to walk the streets. "For approximately half an hour I felt *wonderful*," he told me. "I felt at peace, comfortable, not at all paranoid."

I asked him about passersby. Did they evoke his obsessive concern with the size of his eyes and his penis?

"I didn't even think about it for the whole walk. I looked at people coming toward me on the sidewalk and didn't have any need or urge to glance away. But as soon as I got near the reception, those thoughts did start troubling me—and that was when I realized I had been free for all that time."

Poignantly, he told me that he had never seen the world so clearly as he had for that half-hour—and that since that time he had never felt that way again.

"What way?" I asked him. "If you could sum that good feeling up in one word, what would it be?"

He thought for a while. "Mature," he said. "I actually felt that I could rely on myself to move around in the world and get things done. I felt mature."

The surprising thing about Alan's story is that he never tried to achieve the state again by medicating himself with alcohol on his own. Before his treatment began, however, his social phobia was far too extreme to allow him to take the risk. "What if it didn't work?" he worried. "What if it only got worse?" Research suggests that Alan might indeed have had some realistic cause for concern, since the short-term effect of alcohol ingestion is anxiety reduction but the *long-term* consequences may be actually to increase anxiety symptoms.

CONFLICTING APPROACHES

The special nature of social phobia makes the treatment of alcoholics with social phobia problematic, since Alcoholics Anonymous and other group meetings that are helpful to so many addicts seem specifically designed to inhibit the socially phobic. In most such meetings, it is the custom for members to stand and tell of their drinking problems and struggles. For the socially phobic individual who drinks habitually in the attempt to quell anxiety symptoms, doing that while sober would be completely out of the question.

On the other hand, many drug treatment programs and counselors prohibit the use of all substances they consider mind-altering. In fact, such counselors often target the benzodiazepines—those anxiety drugs mentioned earlier and discussed in detail in the following chapter—viewing them as addicting. This class of medications does cause physiological dependence, but they do not carry the dangers generally associated with addictive drugs: most patients do not tend to take them out of control and/or for recreational purposes. Furthermore, though some argue strenuously to the contrary, the benzodiazepines do not *commonly* lead to alcoholic relapse. Quite the contrary—for many of my patients, these antianxiety drugs have allowed them to quit using alcohol excessively.

One final disagreement arises between anxiety specialists and many drug and alcohol treatment counselors. The latter often resist evidence that suggests that patients may have *two* separate disorders—alcoholism and an anxiety disorder—and that the two may interact with each other. Too often, treatment counselors attribute any anxiety symptoms that arise during the course of treatment to substance withdrawal rather than the emergence of underlying anxiety symptoms. However, the evidence that anxiety is a significant factor is overwhelming: as noted earlier, studies show that about 50 percent of alcoholics meet criteria for at least one anxiety disorder.

In summary, I believe that far too many drug and alcohol treatment programs in this country give patients little or no initial psychiatric evaluation and are poorly grounded in psychological principles. While I agree that it is important to bring substance abuse under control as quickly as possible before psychotherapy and drug therapy can have their beneficial effects, I hope that an increased focus on the role of anxiety disorders will lead to greater cooperation between alcohol programs and other mental health professionals treating anxiety disorders. Given the nature of social phobia, it is hard to imagine a less beneficial position for such a patient than being caught in the cross fire of a professional debate.

Chapter 10

Diagnosis and Treatment

If you are reluctant to ask the way, you will be lost.

—Malay proverb

ANY PSYCHIATRIC CONDITION requires careful evaluation and diagnosis by a mental health practitioner. Although there are some similarities between conditions that affect the body and those that involve the psyche, most of the latter are undetectable by clinical tests. Instead, the experienced clinician is a little like a detective, gathering clues about the patient's inner world. The challenge is twofold: to elicit from the patient a clear and accurate description of those clues—the symptoms—and then to match those symptoms to standardized descriptions of the various and psychiatric conditions—the diagnoses. In effect, diagnoses are nothing but labels for groups of signs and symptoms commonly found together, "boxes" in which clinicians attempt to group cases with similar features.

Given the diversity of human nature, this system is anything but fail-safe. Because patients and their symptoms rarely match the standard categories perfectly, diagnoses are generally imprecise approximations of one individual's particular experience.

But eschewing the standard diagnoses and attempting to treat each disorder as a unique entity would result in complete bedlam. Not only would each clinician need to reinvent the wheel with every patient, but the experiences of other clinicians would be nearly impossible to communicate meaningfully and therefore would be unavailable to the psychiatric community at large. Without a sharing of information, case histories, and other types of clinical experience and insights, individual clinicians would find it all but impossible either to speculate on the cause of a disorder or to decide on a treatment regimen. Imprecise as they may be, the diagnoses listed and described in the revised third edition (1987) of the *Diagnostic and Statistical Manual of Mental Disorders* (abbreviated here as *DSM III-R*), the treatment "bible" of the American Psychiatric Association, give clinicians the many benefits of a shared body of knowledge as well as insights and conclusions gathered and tested over time.

The descriptions in the *DSM III-R* are by no means secret professional knowledge. Although this is a matter of personal preference, once I make a diagnosis, based on a patient's symptoms as well as a thorough medical and psychiatric history, it can be productive and even reassuring for the patient to read and educate him- or herself about the condition. When patients are aware of my diagnosis—the "box" I am using—we can discuss any discrepancies or contradictions and together assess the "fit." Such a discussion can lead to other ideas and possibilities.

Of equal importance is the therapeutic value of diagnosis. Often, people who enter psychotherapy in desperation, unable to control or tolerate their symptoms, experience significant relief simply by learning that their condition is a distinctly recognized disorder shared by many others. Many patients are driven to seek help by the erroneous perception that "something bizarre, unheard of, is happening to me." If the clinician is familiar with the condition and can actually name it and describe a treatment, this note of reassurance is often enough to begin the turnaround toward recovery. The sense of isolation that comes with "it's just me" lifts, visibly lightening the load.

MISDIAGNOSIS AND ANXIETY DISORDERS

Anxiety disorders in general are often misdiagnosed, and this is particularly true in the case of social phobia. There are many reasons for this tendency, but one major factor is the diversity of diagnosticians' background and experience. In today's world, the practice of psychotherapy is by no means restricted to psychiatrists and clinical psychologists, as was the case in the early days of the disciplines. Now the wide spectrum of psychotherapy practitioners includes social workers, nurses, clergypeople, and individuals trained in various forms of counseling. In addition, peer counselors—people who have had personal experience with but no training in treating a particular disorder—abound in alcohol and drug treatment programs. Thus, many people practicing under the rubric of "psychotherapist" may have little or no familiarity with the formal psychiatric diagnostic categories described in the *DSM III-R*. Further, they may have minimal experience with developing the skills involved in reaching an accurate diagnosis.

But psychiatrists and clinical psychologists can misdiagnosis social phobia as well. For those who trained before 1980, when the diagnosis of social phobia first appeared in the *DSM III*, the disorder is not a familiar diagnosis. They might still subscribe to the old belief that anxiety is a nonspecific, broadly "neurotic" condition rather than a group of symptoms specific to particular situations and occurring in particular patterns. In the early 1990s practitioners who have not been specifically trained to recognize and treat anxiety disorders may not consider social anxiety as a possible diagnosis.

A final reason for the widespread misdiagnosis of social anxiety is that the condition is frequently mistaken for or, in some cases, obscured by other anxiety disorders—specifically, panic disorder, panic disorder with agoraphobia, or generalized anxiety disorder. In other instances, social phobia is misdiagnosed as a depressive disorder or a personality disorder such as schizoid or avoidant personality disorder. However, with careful questioning, it is fairly easy to distinguish social phobia from these conditions. Mental health professionals and people who are concerned that they or someone they know might be socially phobic can benefit from a review of the distinctions between social phobia and these various syndromes. Let us take each condition in turn. These disorders are also more fully described in the appendix.

PANIC DISORDER

Mental health professionals are sometimes inadvertently misled when anxiety patients describe themselves as "panicking." In fact, the anxiety associated with social phobia, though it may be extreme, is usually not a discrete panic attack (see table 10.1), although rarely, usually in performance situations, a socially anxious person may experience a true panic attack.

To begin distinguishing panic disorder from social phobia, clinicians can ask whether someone is comfortable being alone. Socially phobic patients tend to be relatively free from anxiety when alone. In fact, unless they are anticipating an upcoming social event, time spent alone or within their families is the only time they are anxiety-free. Patients with panic disorder, however, are typically terrified of being alone and are much comforted by the presence of others.

Another useful question is, "What specifically do you fear will happen?" The root fear for socially phobic people is that others will perceive their anxiety. Those with panic disorder, on the other hand, although sometimes concerned about embarrassment, tend to fear the possibility of attack itself—they have a kind of "fear of fear."

A final question useful for distinguishing the two fears is, "What specifically about crowds or crowded places do you fear?" The social phobic worries about being observed or about meeting someone and being thrown into conversation, while panic patients dread the sense of being closed in, trapped by a crowd and unable to flee. Isaac Marks focused on this distinction when he noted that panic disorder patients fear the crowd while socially phobic people fear the individuals of a crowd.

Studies suggest that between 20 and 50 percent of all social phobics actually suffer from panic disorder as well.[1] In such a case, accurately diagnosing both conditions is essential to designing an effective treatment approach.

TABLE 10.1

Diagnostic Criteria for Panic Disorder

1. The individual experienced one or more unexpected panic attacks (discrete periods of intense fear of discomfort) that were *not* triggered by social situations in which the person was the focus of others' attention.
2. During at least one of the attacks, the person experienced at least four of the following symptoms:

   - Shortness of breath (dyspnea) or the sensations of smothering;
   - Dizziness unsteady feelings, or faintness;
   - Palpitations or accelerated heart rate (tachycardia);
   - Trembling or shaking;
   - Sweating;
   - Choking;
   - Nausea or abdominal distress;
   - Depersonalization or derealization;
   - Numbness or tingling sensations (paresthesia);
   - Flushes (hot flashes) or chills;
   - Chest pain or discomfort;
   - Fear of dying;
   - Fear of going crazy or losing control.

3. Four such attacks have occurred within a four-week period or one or more attacks have been followed by a at least one month of persistent fear of another attack.

Table adapted from American Psychiatric Association, *Diagnostic and Statistical Manual of Mental Disorders,* 3d rev. ed. (Washington, D.C.: American Psychiatric Association, 1987).

PANIC DISORDER WITH AGORAPHOBIA

To further confuse the diagnostic picture, many people with panic disorder develop an extreme fear of having further attacks and, as a result, become phobic in certain situations (see table 10.1). Thus, it is not uncommon for the person with agoraphobia resulting from panic disorder to fear such crowded places as theaters, shopping malls, grocery stores, churches, concerts, buses, trains, airplanes, and even traffic jams in cars. In response, as described in chapter 1, they may constrict their activities markedly—just as social phobics do in order to avoid social interaction.

However, although the resulting social isolation might be identical, the underlying fears are quite different. For example, people with agoraphobia may fear riding on public transportation because they lack control there and could become "trapped" if an attack should occur. Conversely, a person with social anxiety would be likely to avoid public transportation in order to avoid coming under the scrutiny of other passengers or being compelled to make small talk. Probing for answers as to what *precisely* one fears as well as pursuing the questions listed earlier, for panic disorder, is a way of tapping the underlying reasons for similar fear responses.

GENERALIZED ANXIETY DISORDER

Some people tend to feel "keyed up" all the time and to respond to life's stresses with a variety of physical symptoms; they suffer from generalized anxiety disorder (GAD). Their symptoms are related to the autonomic arousal that is the hallmark of the social phobic (see the appendix). Again, specific questions reveal that social phobics' concerns and symptoms are confined to specific social or performance situations, whereas the symptoms of GAD arise in response to a broad range of stressful life activities. Also, although GAD patients tend to suffer with the disorder for years, their lives are usually impaired only mildly and, in contrast to social phobics, they are usually able to continue their activities despite their continuing distress (see table 10.2).

TABLE 10.2

Diagnostic Criteria for Generalized Anxiety Disorder

1. The person experienced unrealistic or excessive anxiety and worry (apprehensive expectation) about two or more life circumstances—for example, worry about possible misfortune to one's child (who is in no danger) and worry about finances (for no good reason), for a period of six months or longer, during which the person was bothered more days than not by these concerns.

2. At least six of the following eighteen symptoms are often present when anxious:

MOTOR TENSION
- Trembling, twitching, or feeling shaky;
- Muscle tension, aches, or soreness;
- Restlessness;
- Easy fatigability.

AUTONOMIC HYPERACTIVITY
- Shortness of breath or smothering sensations;
- Palpitations or accelerated heart rate (tachycardia);
- Sweating, or cold clammy hands;
- Dry mouth;
- Dizziness or lightheadedness;
- Nausea, diarrhea, or other abdominal distress;
- Flushes (hot flashes) or chills;
- Frequent urination;
- Trouble swallowing or "lump in throat."

VIGILANCE AND SCANNING
- Feeling keyed up or on edge;
- Exaggerated startle response;
- Difficulty concentrating or "mind going blank" because of anxiety;
- Trouble falling or staying asleep;
- Irritability.

Table adapted from American Psychiatric Association, *Diagnostic and Statistical Manual of Mental Disorders,* 3d rev. ed. (Washington, D.C.: American Psychiatric Association, 1987).

DEPRESSION

On the surface, the typical picture of depression does not resemble social phobia, although both may be accompanied by feelings of worthlessness and indecisiveness or nonassertiveness. Commonly, however, such a patient is clearly suffering from a major depressive disorder that obscures an underlying social phobia. In such a case, the result of the dual conditions is an intensification of the assault on self-esteem, initiative, and communication. As a result, these individuals become isolated, intensely lonely, bereft of social relationships and even human contact. If the social phobia remains unrecognized and the patient is treated for depression alone, any possible improvement may be only temporary. And if, in this case, medication is used to treat the depression, the pharmacological decisions may be completely ineffective in treating the hidden social phobia.

Marge, a thirty-seven-year-old divorced postal worker had been hospitalized for depression and suicidal feelings on three different occasions over the seven years before our first session. Despite the fact that she had been in psychotherapy for a long time, she came to our clinic after seeing a newspaper article on social phobia. "It described me to a T," she told me. "Since my divorce, I have had no life—I go to work and come home. I can't stand being with people, particularly if I have to meet new people, and men scare me to death. Living such an empty life, my self-esteem bottoms out and I feel that there is nothing to do but kill myself. Then my therapist talks me into going to the hospital, I get treated for depression, and then I go home. But nothing changes."

Marge's therapist had based her treatment on the assumption that her isolation and avoidance were due to chronic depression. Her antidepressant medication did alleviate some depressive symptoms, but it was not effective at all in treating Marge's social anxiety. Marge's recovery depended on a fuller diagnosis and treatment plan that encompassed the full range of her symptoms. It is important that *both* disorders be diagnosed and treated. See table 10.3 for the diagnostic criteria for major depressive disorder.

TABLE 10.3

Diagnostic Criteria for Major Depressive Disorder

The presence of *five* of the following symptoms during the same two-week period, representing a change from previous function:

1. Depressed mood (or irritability in children and adolescents) most of the day nearly every day, as indicated either by self-report or others' observation;
2. Markedly diminished interest or pleasure in all, or almost all, activities most of the day nearly every day (as indicated either by self-report or others' observation);
3. Significant weight loss or weight gain (5 percent of body weight or more in a month) without dieting, or a decrease or increase in appetite nearly every day (in children this would be a failure to make expected weight gains);
4. Insomnia or hypersomnia (too much sleep) nearly every day;
5. Psychomotor agitation or retardation nearly every day (observable by others; not merely subjective feelings of restlessness or slowness);
6. Fatigue or loss of energy nearly every day;
7. Feelings of worthlessness or excessive or inappropriate guilt (not merely self-reproach or guilt about being sick);
8. A diminished ability to think, concentrate, or make decisions nearly every day (evidenced either by self-report or others' observation);
9. Recurrent thoughts of death (not just fears of dying), recurrent ideas of suicide without a specific plan.

Table adapted from American Psychiatric Association, *Diagnostic and Statistical Manual of Mental Disorders,* 3d rev. ed. (Washington, D.C.: American Psychiatric Association, 1987).

PERSONALITY DISORDERS

Personality disorders in general are longstanding abnormal patterns of perceiving, relating to, and thinking about the world and oneself. People diagnosed with these disorders generally

consider the traits that distinguish them natural and normal
("this is me, that's how I am"), and many clinicians consider personality disorders to be relatively unchangeable through treatment. Therefore, a person diagnosed with a personality disorder
is likely to receive less aggressive specific treatment than one
with another diagnosis.

In our clinic, I have seen social phobia misdiagnosed as one
of two different personality disorders—schizoid personality or
avoidant personality. The diagnosis of schizoid personality
describes a person who is solitary, with no close friends or confidants, and a restricted range of emotional experience and
expression. People with this disorder neither desire nor enjoy
close relationships, have little desire for sexual experiences, and
are largely indifferent to praise or criticism. Whereas a social
phobic may wish desperately for social relationships, the
schizoid person prefers to be alone.

A more common misdiagnosis is avoidant personality disorder, the distinctive feature of which is pervasive social discomfort. As table 10.4 shows, this diagnosis covers practically all the
symptoms of generalized social phobia, but includes some addi-
tional features as well. There is considerable debate as to
whether avoidant personality is simply a severe social phobia—a
position I tend to favor—or a completely distinct condition. It
appears that clinicians tend to make this diagnosis more often in
the cases of men, especially if they have poor social skills and
come from lower socioeconomic strata, a bias that can be down-
right destructive if it allows social phobia to go untreated.

However, the literature on the subject and our own experience in the anxiety clinic suggests that treatments that are
effective for social phobia are also useful with avoidant personality. It is likely that the psychiatric community as a whole will
soon begin to perceive avoidant personality to represent the
severe end of a continuum that begins with common shyness
and has as its middle ground social anxiety merging into social
phobia.

TABLE 10.4

Diagnostic Criteria for Avoidant Personality Disorder

A pervasive pattern of social discomfort, fear of negative evaluation, and timidity, beginning by early adulthood and present in a variety of contexts, as indicated by at least four of the following:

1. Is easily hurt by criticism or disapproval;
2. Has no close friends or confidants (or only one) other than first-degree relatives;
3. Is unwilling to become involved with people unless is certain of being liked;
4. Avoids social or occupational activities that involve significant inter-personal contact;
5. Is reticent in social situations because of a fear of saying something inappropriate or foolish or of being unable to answer a question;
6. Fears being embarrassed by blushing, crying, or showing signs of anxiety in front of other people;
7. Exaggerates the potential difficulties, physical dangers, or risks involved in doing something ordinary but outside the usual routine.

Table adapted from American Psychiatric Association, *Diagnostic and Statistical Manual of Mental Disorders*, 3d rev. ed. (Washington, D.C.: American Psychiatric Association, 1987).

THE BRIEF SOCIAL PHOBIA SCALE

Table 10.5 is the Brief Social Phobia Scale, a diagnostic tool developed by the psychiatrist Jonathan Davidson, who is the director of the Anxiety and Traumatic Stress Program at Duke University. If you or someone you know suspects social phobia as a diagnosis, this short test will give you a general idea as to how closely it conforms to the standard diagnostic criteria. To use the scale, rate each of the symptoms according to the given ratings; then total all the scores. Note that there is no absolute score that indicates social phobia. As a point of comparison, it is useful to know that Davidson's patients in a treatment study

TABLE 10.5

The Brief Social Phobia Scale

Part I: Fear and Avoidance

How much do you fear and avoid the following situations? Please give separate ratings for fear and avoidance.

Fear Rating	Avoidance Rating
0 = None	0 = None
1 = Mild	1 = Rare
2 = Moderate	2 = Sometimes
3 = Severe	3 = Extreme
4 = Extreme	4 = Always

	Fear	Avoidance
Speaking in public or in front of others	_____	_____
Talking to people in authority	_____	_____
Talking to strangers	_____	_____
Being embarrassed or humiliated	_____	_____
Being criticized	_____	_____
Social gatherings	_____	_____
Doing something while being watched (this does not include speaking)	_____	_____

Part II: Physiologic

When you are in a situation that involves contact with other people, or when you are thinking about such a situation, do you experience the following symptoms?

Rating
0 = None
1 = Mild
2 = Moderate
3 = Severe
4 = Extreme

Blushing	_____	Trembling	_____
Palpitations	_____	Sweating	_____

Fear = _____ Avoidance = _____ Physiologic = _____ Total = _____

Table adapted from J. R. T. Davidson, N. L. S. Potts, E. A. Richichi, S. M. Ford, K. R. R. Krishman, R.D. Smith, and W. Wilson, "The Brief Social Phobia Scale," *Journal of Clinical Psychiatry* 52, no. 11 (1991 suppl.): 48–51.

for social phobia had pretreatment scores on this scale ranging from 19 to 56, with an average of 40. But be cautioned: these were the scores of people deemed by one research group to be socially phobic enough to require medication.[2] In no way do I mean to imply that all people scoring in this range are socially phobic or should be treated with medications. Remember, only a qualified and experienced clinician can make an accurate diagnosis.

SURVEYING TREATMENTS

This is not a self-help book. Most people with severe social phobia require professional help. The patients I have seen and written about in this book struggled for many years on their own, going from one to another "popular psychology" approach without success. This is not to say that there are no helpful measures that sufferers of social phobia can initiate on their own, but ineffective attempts at self-treatment may only delay solutions for a problem that can be effectively treated with the proper specific approach.

In our clinic, we often encourage our socially phobic patients—particularly those whose fears are relatively circumscribed, such as public speaking—to force themselves to become active in settings and organizations that require social contact. These might include formal organizations, interest-oriented groups that center on something close to the person's heart, or even the famous Dale Carnegie speech courses, which have helped millions of people overcome their fears of public speaking. In general, it is helpful to confront the behaviors that one avoids, since doing more of what is feared often, though not always, tends to reduce anxiety. For readers who believe that they might be socially phobic, it would certainly not hurt to attempt to overcome the phobia by increasing social contact. Obviously, though, for some people this will be impossible.

WHEN TO SEEK HELP

Only sufferers themselves can ultimately decide whether their social discomfort is intense enough to warrant the time, cost, effort, and inevitable discomfort of self-disclosure involved in treatment. Whether or not the person's condition strictly meets the criteria for social phobia is irrelevant to the decision of whether or not to seek help.

Once the decision is made to get help, however, several barriers still remain. The first is the enduring stigma in our society attached to mental and emotional problems. Although some progress has been made, many people continue to view mental disorders as merely deficits of will power. Typically, socially phobic individuals not only face the inherent difficulty of approaching and engaging in complex interactions with people considered authorities, but they also brave imagined judgments about their "silly" problem, one they themselves generally feel they "should be able to get over." As more than one of my patients has said to me, marveling at the progress they have made, "Before I came here I thought I would rather die than talk about my problems the way I talk about them with you, but now I do things, I have initiative for social encounters—I'm not just passively responding anymore."

Another major obstacle, and one that I hope this book will help eliminate, is the failure of sufferers and those concerned about them to recognize the condition for what it is. Many people who have been socially anxious and inhibited for most of their lives grow to consider this condition "normal," an integral part of their personalities and not a treatable condition. This is particularly true for those who have been able to arrange their lives in order to avoid feared situations. Such was the case for Barbara, a lawyer who had been referred to me several years ago for the treatment of depression. She had lost both her mother and sister the year before, and was extremely despondent. The therapist who referred her to me had asked if I would consider prescribing an antidepressant. After taking a brief history, I agreed, prescribing fluoxetine, better known as

Prozac (discussed later more fully). Barbara responded well to this treatment, returning to her nondepressed state while continuing her grieving work with her therapist. At a follow-up visit approximately a year later, I suggested that she begin easing off the medication. "Please, no," she cried. "I'm just beginning to live!"

To my surprise, she described a variety of socially phobic symptoms and avoidance behaviors that had been pervasive in her life but that she had neglected to mention to me. I had missed them in my brief evaluation of her depression, partly because I had not been looking for them and partly because she was relatively unaware of them herself. "I never realized what a constricted and fearful life I was leading," she told me. "I avoided parties, social contacts of all kinds, speaking up even in situations where it was important professionally that I do so. I'd been going on so long that way that I hardly noticed. But now every day is a surprise for me—a *pleasant* surprise. I'm part of the world again: twice as effective as an attorney and having a really good time."

"Understanding" spouses, supportive relatives or friends, and jobs that require little social interaction may even allow the socially anxious to "forget" their problem and avoid perceiving how constricted their lives have become. As many of the examples in this book demonstrate, it is often a forced change in life pattern that causes these people to seek help. For people not jarred into self-assessment in this way, it takes a careful and objective assessment to realize the extent to which opportunities have been passed up or goals abandoned.

WHAT KIND OF HELP?

A number of treatment options for social phobia exist or are being developed, but at this point few have been tested in controlled studies to demonstrate clear effectiveness. Even the literature on shyness, which is full of "soft" suggestions on how to change, lacks support for the efficacy of the advice. However, a consensus is developing among practicing clinicians as to what actually works for this anxiety disorder, and our experiences in the anxiety clinic are consistent with these emerging conclusions. These treatment options are of two types—psychotherapeutic and pharmacological. These can be pursued individually but they are often best combined.

PSYCHOTHERAPIES

It is important to state at the outset that only certain kinds of psychotherapy appear to have a significant impact on social phobia, and these do *not* include the general, nonspecific forms of psychotherapy. By "general," I mean the forms of therapy commonly referred to as "psychodynamic" and those quite broadly called "counseling." These include approaches that involve extensive reviews of childhood experiences, searches for unconscious motivations, and explorations of the symbolic meaning of certain behaviors. Although these therapies have other uses, socially phobic patients who have been in general psychotherapy commonly describe themselves as becoming increasingly comfortable with their therapists but *only* with their therapists. Outside the sessions, the social anxiety remains as crippling as ever.

Social Skills Training

Several specific types of therapy have had mixed success with socially anxious people. Social skills training, for example, assumes that patients with social phobia lack basic social techniques—that is, they simply do not *know* how to act. The primary goal is to teach and aid them in practicing effective social behaviors. This type of therapy involves mixtures of such techniques as rehearsal, modeling, role playing with feedback sessions, and homework assignments—for example, "This week comment on the weather to someone on your bus," or "This week, smile and compliment someone at work on what he or she is wearing." Such task-oriented intervention can be quite useful for some, but it is becoming increasingly apparent that most people with social phobia do not really lack basic social skills but rather are constrained from practicing them by fear, negative thoughts, and avoidance.

Exposure Therapy: Confronting One's Fears

Another approach, proven effective in the treatment of phobias, is exposure therapy, sometimes called desensitization. This treatment is specifically designed to accustom the patient gradually to a particular feared situation. The underlying principle is that repeated exposure to feared stimuli over time will cause a reduction in the fearful response and a diminution of anxiety symptoms. Exposure therapy is most effective for simple phobias and agoraphobia.

A good example of exposure therapy is found in the treatment of spider phobia. Let us say, for example, that Margaret is petrified by spiders to the point that she is unable to leave a sidewalk and walk on a path, even a paved path, that divides a lawn. And even when she is safe at home she is so filled with anticipatory anxiety about seeing a spider that she is no longer able to leave her house and enter other houses or buildings. To begin treating her, a therapist asks her to help develop a hierarchy, a series of graduated exposures to spiders, that would lead her in small steps into close proximity with one. Margaret begins her hierarchy by assigning herself the task of simply writing the word *spider* repetitively. Then she moves to the viewing of pictures of spiders in books. Next, she is shown a spider in a transparent box, first from a distance and then at increasingly closer distances. With each step, the therapist stays close by and encourages Margaret to remain at that level—to repeat the prescribed behavior over and over—until anxiety diminishes. Eventually, Margaret can sit with relative ease in a room where a spider is placed on the arm of her chair.

Exposure therapy is remarkably effective in treating simple phobias such as Margaret's. At the end of such a program of gradations, many of our clinic patients are able to remain relatively anxiety-free in proximity with the object of their fear. Similarly, agoraphobics who were unable before therapy to leave their homes are able, after repeated guided exposures first to the front lawn, then to the street corner, then perhaps to the small shop a block away, and so forth, to become capable of loosening the constraints on their lives.

It seemed natural that exposure therapy would be useful for social phobia, and so far results suggest that it is valuable for some aspects, particularly discrete, circumscribed social fears. Dale Carnegie courses and public speaking opportunities all rely on this element. For example, patients with a fear of writing in front of others benefit from a graduated series of exposures with their therapists' encouragement. Perhaps they are assigned the task of buying items with a credit card, buying travelers' checks at a bank, or paying for items with a check—all with the support and presence of the therapist—first in a practice situation on the site where the activity will take place and then in the real-life circumstance (found to be more effective than practice in the shelter of a therapist's office). People who fear eating in restaurants may begin by entering and leaving, next buying something to go, then progressing to a cup of coffee, and finally graduate to a full meal.

But for generalized social phobia, exposure therapy is less useful. First, it is difficult to set up and control predictable situations that can be graded to match the patient's anxiety level. Also, there are ways to sabotage the therapy by being in situations without actually "being there." Recall Amy, for example, who was able to contain her anxiety by pretending that she was merely carrying out the role of "playing receptionist." Others "put on an act"; if they pretend they are someone or even somewhere else, they can diminish their anxiety. Still others play only a passive role in social interaction, unable to contribute to a conversation except as responders. One of our patients routinely accepted all social invitations but would seek out her hosts' children immediately upon entering in order to engage them in conversation. She found them less threatening than adults, and thus escaped the need to socialize with other guests. If children were not present, she would often strike up conversations with the bartender or kitchen help—again, people she viewed as less threatening than her peers. These kinds of maneuvers had become so habitual that she considered herself a fairly outgoing person. It took careful, detailed probing on the therapist's part to isolate her social fears. All such avoidance behaviors neutralize the effectiveness of exposure therapy, since they prevent the person from being fully engaged.

Apparently, too, the negative thoughts characteristic of social phobia are often powerful enough to override any benefit that repeated exposures might have. For example, people who are unable to enter rooms because they fear negative judgment from those inside may not experience the positive effects of repeatedly doing so. Their beliefs about the possible scrutiny and consequent humiliation they face can be far stronger than the effect of gradual exposure. This failure of exposure therapy provides a clue to an alternative treatment. It appears that the cognitive component of social phobia is so strong that it calls for specific attention in the therapeutic approach.

Cognitive Therapy

Cognitive therapy, made famous by the psychologist Aaron Beck originally for depression, assumes that anxiety results from the patient's mistaken appraisal of a situation.[3] The challenge to the patient in this form of therapy involves collaborating with the therapist to identify and change mistaken thoughts that inhibit normal functioning. The central premise, then, is that one can learn more effective ways of coping with anxiety.

Successful therapy combines the fundamentals of cognitive therapy with exposure therapy to form an effective treatment approach to social phobia. First, the therapist helps the patient identify breaches of logic or groundless assumptions in his or her thinking: for example, "I know they think I'm a stupid fool" (mind reading); "If I speak, the man who seems to know every-thing here will just get up and walk away" (fortune-telling); "If they see how nervous I am they'll laugh at me and tell my boss and I will lose my job" (catastrophizing); or "Either she'll fall in love with me or she'll never talk to me again" (all-or-nothing thinking). Social phobics al.. frequently engage in "selective remembering"—retaining memories of their social failures but forgetting or failing to recognize their successes.

In cognitive therapy, the therapist helps a person first recog-nize and then restructure or control such maladaptive thought processes, often through homework assignments and diary keep-ing. For example, a graduate student who found it difficult to enter a classroom was encouraged to actively notice who looked up when he went in and what their facial expressions conveyed. He was also asked to observe responses that the meeting partici-pants had to *others* who entered the room late. In the course of this assignment, he had to admit that virtually everyone looked uninterested when he entered—and it came as a great surprise to him to realize that his anxiety was resting on a mistaken assumption.

Another case involved Brad, a junior executive in a consult-ing firm. He was treated by my colleague Tim Strauman, who specializes in cognitive behavior therapy. Brad was having a terri-ble time speaking up at meetings at work. Each time he had to participate, he wound up so preoccupied with his colleagues' judgments of him—negative judgments, he was certain—that he was completely oblivious to the business being transacted.

In a typical first step in the cognitive approach, Dr. Strauman asked Brad to focus on the thoughts that passed through his mind during meetings. His self-talk was characteristically socially anxious—for example, "I'm making a terrible impression," "That guy isn't listening to me—he's smirking!" "If I make a mistake my co-workers will think I'm totally incompetent. They'll see that I'm nervous and think there's something wrong with me."

Once Brad became aware of his thoughts, he was able to gain a certain amount of control over them, which went some distance toward reducing his anxiety. With Dr. Strauman's help, he examined each statement or belief and as an exercise asked himself, "What evidence do I have that the belief or statement is true?" As with many other social phobics, Brad's most unflattering assumptions were completely unsupported. For example, though he believed others saw him as nervous, his co-workers often remarked that he seemed quite articulate and knowledgeable at meetings. In rational terms, it was unlikely that one slip would alter this general impression. Besides, as time went on, Brad came to realize that he was holding himself to a much more exacting standard than others used, and even that he, himself, applied to others.

As Brad began to examine his fears and assumptions, he came to see how extreme and biased they were. Over time, with the aid of experiments that he helped Dr. Strauman devise in which he *intentionally* used the wrong word or hesitated during a conversation, Brad began to see that his catastrophic expectations about "screwing up" were exaggerated and contributing substantially to his anxiety. He and Dr. Strauman began to work on substituting the biased, exaggerated thoughts with more realistic ones—for example, "Most people do not expect perfection from me" and "It is unlikely that I will be instantly and permanently judged as incompetent if I make a mistake during a sales presentation." Also, by developing his observation skills under Dr. Strauman's direction, Brad began to recognize that others rarely noticed his anxiety, and even when they did, no dire consequences followed. In this way, cognitive therapy provides the opportunity to interrupt automatic thoughts and evaluate them, replacing them if necessary with more realistic responses to social situations.

The psychologist R. J. Heimberg and his group at the State University of New York at Albany discovered that the cognitive/exposure approach was most effective in small groups composed of people with similar problems.[4] Everyone in a group of social phobics benefits from knowing that each of the members has similar anxieties and difficulties, and in our clinic we have seen lively discussions and feelings of generous support develop among people who, in other circumstances, have been unable to conduct a conversation. In the safety of such a group, they are able to practice, share experiences, perform, and offer feedback to others—all unique experiences for many socially phobic patients.

This combined approach is currently being developed and refined, and it may be difficult to find a therapist who specializes in these techniques. For help in finding a psychotherapist familiar with this strategy, contact the National Anxiety Disorders Association of America, 6000 Executive Boulevard, Suite 200, Rockville, MD 20852-3901.

PHARMACOLOGICAL TREATMENT

In general, for most psychiatric conditions that are responsive to drug therapy, integrating a psychological treatment with a pharmacologic one is almost always more effective than either form of therapy alone. It is important to note, however, that for social phobia the effectiveness of combination therapy has not been proved to be greater than drug therapy alone—though most of us working in the field believe it to be. Rather tentatively, I began prescribing medications, reassured by several small studies in the literature that reported some rather dramatic results. I do prescribe medications alone, but more often I include them in a combined treatment program.

As with all medical conditions, the decision as to whether or not to use medications rests on a risk/benefit appraisal. This decision-making process involves a careful assessment by the patient and physicians regarding the impact of the phobia upon the patient's life. How great is the impairment and how great are the medications' risks? Fortunately, the medications that are effective for social phobia are safe when properly used.

That said, I am reminded of the psychiatrist Peter Kramer's recent book, *Listening to Prozac*, in which he describes his awe of the dramatic changes his patients experienced in response to the medication fluoxetine (Prozac). He was treating his patients for depression, but he noticed impressive alterations in the feelings and behaviors of many, and noted seeming personality changes in response to the medication.[5] I have seen similar changes, just as dramatic, in treating social phobia with medications alone.

This is certainly not always the case, but sometimes the responses—behavior changes, even *life* changes—astound me. I have mixed feelings about mentioning these intense turn-arounds, since I do not wish to suggest that I am overly enamored of medications and tout them indiscriminately. In the pages that follow, as I discuss specific drugs, I will describe several of these dramatic responses. Remember, however, that in most cases improvement as a result of drug therapy is more modest. Table 10.6 lists some of the drugs used to treat social phobia.

TABLE 10.6

Drugs Used in Social Phobia Treatment

GENERIC NAME	BRAND NAME	USUAL DOSE RANGE
Beta Blockers		
Propranolol	Inderal	20–40 mg/dose
Atenolol	Tenormin	50–100 mg/day
MAOIs		
Phenelzine	Nardil	45–105 mg/day
Tranylcypromine	Parnate	30–60 mg/day
Benzodiazepines		
Clonazepam	Klonopin	1–5 mg/day
Alprazolam	Xanax	2–8 mg/day
Others		
Fluoxetine	Prozac	20–80 mg/day

Beta Blockers

The class of medications called beta blockers has traditionally been used to treat cardiovascular conditions such as hypertension (high blood pressure) or to suppress irregular heart rhythms. These medications exert their effect on the autonomic system to dampen symptoms such as sweating, tremor, palpitations, and rapid heart rate. Because these are common symptoms of anxiety, it did not take long before beta blockers were prescribed for anxiety disorders to reduce autonomic arousal in anxiety-producing situations. In fact, the first widespread use in this way developed as a result of an underground traffic in beta blockers among performing artists, largely without the supervision of physicians. Subsequently, formal studies found this class of drugs to be useful in performance-type situations.[6] Julie, described in chapter 1, successfully used a beta blocker along with rehearsals and several sessions of cognitive therapy to present her work orally in her final university course. Another patient uses beta blockers before monthly lunch meetings with fellow faculty members. Several executives treated at our clinic use these drugs before giving quaterly reports to company superiors.

Beta blockers appear to work by diminishing the individual's anxiety-related symptoms that are interpreted as evidence of distress. As a result, they appear to interrupt the vicious cycle of feeling anxious, perceiving physical symptoms, and consequently spiraling into more anxiety. The medication is commonly taken several hours before the anticipated event.

One patient who uses a beta blocker successfully in making presentations at work describes its effects this way: "I feel steadier, my heart is not coming out of my chest, and I know that I am not likely to shake. It gives me confidence that I will not look anxious and I can concentrate on my speaking." Others note "it takes the edge off" or "I don't feel so wrought up. My body won't give me away."

We commonly use propranolol (Inderal) or a longer-acting beta blocker, atenolol (Tenormin). While they are helpful for specific situations, beta blockers as a class have not proven particularly useful for generalized social phobia. Using them "as needed" is difficult for people who are phobic in a broad range of social situations. Also, when these drugs are used regularly, their beneficial effects appear to diminish, whether this is due to tolerance or dependence, the reasons are not clear.

But for people with localized social fears, these medications, used properly under medical supervision, are safe. The side effects are relatively minimal—occasionally there is a sense of lethargy, fatigue, or feelings of light-headedness after standing up abruptly, but these seem to fade with use. However, people with asthma, congestive heart failure, or a history of allergies that cause wheezing should not take beta blockers.[6]

Monoamine-Oxidase Inhibitors

In a program to treat certain kinds of depression with monoamine-oxidase inhibiting drugs (MAOIs), the psychiatrist Michael Liebowitz and his colleagues at Columbia University noted that whereas before their patients were hypersensitive to criticism, were easily hurt by others' comments, and had frequent mood swings, the MAOIs seemed to alleviate these uncomfortable feelings. In assessing these changes, the psychiatrists hypothesized that this class of medications might prove useful for social anxiety as well.[7] In a related controlled clinical study, they found that indeed most of the socially anxious patients treated with the MAOIs reported increased confidence, a higher resistance to criticism, and reduced anxiety during social or performance situations. In fact, these patients experienced an overall reduction in distress both in purely social situations and in their jobs. (The psychiatrists also found that a beta blocker was relatively ineffective for their subjects with generalized social phobia.)[8] The MAOI used most commonly in studies and in our clinic is phenelzine (Nardil). Tranylcypromine (Parnate) is another drug in this family that has been shown to be effective.

The MAOIs appear to work by preventing neurotransmitter breakdown in the central nervous system; the result is an elevation in the levels of the neurotransmitters norepinephrine, serotonin, and particularly dopamine. Exactly why dopamine and the other neurotransmitters reduce the symptoms of social phobia is unknown. It may be that in addition to reducing the pain of rejection or personal criticism, a boost in the presence of these chemicals may increase the pleasurable feelings that are the reward for successful social interaction.

In terms of safety, however, this class of drugs needs more than the usual amount of care—the physician must take care to prescribe correctly and to educate the patient fully about use, and the patient must take care to comply precisely with the physician's instructions. These drugs can react with a chemical in certain foods or with other medications to raise the blood pressure sharply. Although this is rare, it could result in a dangerous hypertensive crisis. Pharmacists dispensing these drugs should provide patients with a list of foods and drugs to be avoided.

Other common side effects are drowsiness, dry mouth, and weight gain. If they occur at all, these effects tend to be mild to moderate and often subside as treatment continues. Overall, with the proper precautions, the drugs are safe—and their benefits to socially phobic patients can be very dramatic.

David, the neurologist described in chapter 1, exhibited one of the most memorable turnarounds I have ever seen after I prescribed a regimen of the MAOI phenelzine (Nardil). Several weeks after he began taking the drug, he reported feeling "like a new person." He noted that he could now look people in the eye, actually enjoyed seeking out and initiating conversations, and in general felt more confident. After several more weeks, in a follow-up phone call, he told me, "My wife is calling me a social animal. I'm actually looking forward to those Friday nights at the country club, and we've begun to have small dinners and large cocktail parties at our house. My wife has been wanting to do that for many years, but I could never face the idea."

"It's really been that dramatic?" I asked, with some skepticism.

"Here, let me put my nurse on—she runs the office."

The nurse was enthusiastic. "He is a completely different person," she told me. "Patients now comment on how much more outgoing and friendly he is. His personality change has had a positive effect on the whole office."

The therapeutic effect of a MAOI is seldom this spectacular, although my patients and I are often surprised at how greatly it alters what they have come to consider permanent personality traits. Increased confidence, lowered social fearfulness, and a substantial reduction of avoidant behavior are all common responses to this family of drugs.

Studies are under way on a promising new type of MAOI not yet available in the United States. One of these, a drug called moclobemide, is a reversible inhibitor of monoamine-oxidase that does not require dietary restrictions.

Remember that it is important to differentiate depression from social phobia, because some of the traditional antidepressant medications—for example, the tricyclic group such as imipramine (Tofranil), amitriptyline (Elavil), and nortriptyline (Pamelor)—are not useful for social phobia. Several small studies document the successful use of fluoxetine (Prozac), another popular antidepressant, in treating both social phobia and avoidant personality disorder.[9] In the clinic, our experience with using Prozac for social phobia was mixed—when successful, it is often quite useful, but it is less often helpful than either the MAOIs or certain of the benzodiazepines.

Benzodiazepines

Another class of medications, specifically designed to treat anxiety, has proved very useful in treating social phobia. These are the benzodiazepines, whose most famous representatives are diazepam (Valium) and chlordiazepoxide (Librium). Other very useful additions to the group are lorazepam (Ativan) and alprazolam (Xanax). Another is clonazepam (Klonopin), a drug used for years as an anticonvulsant and recently "rediscovered" for use with anxiety.

We probably know more about the action of benzodiazepines than any other psychoactive drugs—in fact, more than about most drugs used in medicine. In 1977, it was discovered that specific benzodiazepine receptors exist in the brain, and since that time a search has been ongoing for a natural benzodiazepine that would explain their existence. When the drug molecules bind to these receptors in the brain, a neurotransmitter called gamma-aminobutyric acid is triggered that inhibits neurons in the areas of the brain that produce anxiety.

Benzodiazepines have been used successfully in such anxiety disorders as generalized anxiety and panic disorder, suggesting that they might be useful in treating social phobia. Two drugs have been studied in this regard—alprazolam and clonazepam. In the largest study, of clonazepam in 1991, Davidson and his colleagues reported that 84 percent of their socially phobic patients showed "good improvement" in response to treatment with the drug.[10]

An example demonstrates the effect this drug can have. Jason, a thirty-four-year-old computer expert, was unable to work while others were watching. This was a severe handicap in his job, since part of his responsibility involved teaching, often through the demonstration of various facets of computer programming and operation. In anticipation of these sessions, Jason would tremble and perspire, sometimes for days, and when he came in for treatment he was no longer able to operate a computer in the presence of others for fear of having his tremor or perspiration observed. He tried to compensate by standing behind students and giving instructions, but there were times when demonstration was unavoidable. However, after several weeks of treatment with clonazepam, Jason reported full recovery. "I'm just not afraid at all. I don't worry about the sessions beforehand and I find myself doing things naturally, without worrying about seizing up. I really believe that this medication has saved my career. I was considering retraining, but now I'm completely at ease."

After a moment, he continued, "You know, I actually volunteered to teach a seminar. I can't believe it." This was a significant realization, since anxiety patients often need encouragement to challenge their early fears. It is for this reason, among others, that appropriate psychotherapy is a desirable adjunct to even the most effective drug treatment. This is true for any of the medications used for social phobia. Patients are frequently surprised that they are able to do the things they have avoided doing for years, but they may not try them without specific encouragement. In some basic way, they have to "relearn" the fact that the pain is gone in each new formerly feared situation.

The Benzodiazepine Controversy

The benzodiazepines have come in for a great deal of media attention in the recent past—newspaper and magazine articles and television reports that have sown as much misinformation as clarity. Let me be clear from the outset about where I stand in this ongoing controversy. In my view, the benzodiazepines are a remarkable category of medicine—useful over a broad spectrum of distresses, they are very safe. Unless other drugs are involved, it is highly unusual for this category of drugs to be associated with a death even when they are taken in huge overdoses. For this reason, they have replaced a category of highly addicting, very dangerous drugs whose use was once widespread; these included meprobamate, the barbiturates, and other kinds of sedatives, all of which were associated with countless fatalities.

Despite this shift, there remains much stigma and ignorance about the use of benzodiazepines both among professionals and the general public. Partly these assumptions result from the massive abuses of Valium and the severe withdrawal effects that followed discontinuation of large doses of Valium reported during the 1960s and 1970s. Another surge of press attention resulted from the enthusiasm over Xanax, a benzodiazepine often prescribed for panic disorder. The charge against Xanax, too, has been that it is an addictive drug and therefore an unacceptable tradeoff regardless of its benefits.

The term *addiction* denotes a substance that causes dysfunction or impairment, causes the development of an ever-increasing tolerance (meaning that one must take increasingly large doses to achieve the same effect), and/or that causes "drug seeking" behaviors. None of these characteristics are particularly true of benzodiazepines when prescribed for anxiety patients who do not have a substantial history of drug or alcohol abuse.

It is true, however, that patients may develop what is called a physiologic dependence on benzodiazepines—that is, the body "gets used to them"—if they are used for prolonged periods, and if the medication is withdrawn abruptly, the central nervous system's receptors "protest," resulting in withdrawal symptoms. In fact, almost every medication that affects the central nervous system entails this sort of "down-regulation," and all such drugs must be both administered and withdrawn only under strict medical supervision.

Where medications that produce dependence are withdrawn too abruptly, withdrawal symptoms occur that mimic anxiety. Unless the medication is reduced slowly, it is difficult to tell whether the underlying anxiety symptoms are returning or a withdrawal phenomenon is occurring. However, neither response is evidence of drug "addiction," and anyone—be it the patient, the doctor, the therapist, the patient's spouse, or another observer—who suggests that a patient is addicted who takes appropriately prescribed amounts under supervision is misusing the term.

As I indicated in chapter 9, when patients have drug and alcohol histories in addition to anxiety disorders, treatment with benzodiazepines grows more complicated. Here the clinician is challenged with sorting through the "chicken/egg" phenomenon: is the patient drinking or taking drugs in the effort to self-medicate against an underlying anxiety condition? Would treating the anxiety condition aid in abstinence from the drug or alcohol? Clinicians and patients need to face these questions together and to develop a treatment regimen that takes this possibility into account.

Two other side effects in treatment with benzodiazepine have received a great deal of attention, far more than is warranted in terms of their long-term significance. With high doses, memory problems or slight motor incoordination can occur. These too are usually mild effects and often clear with time. And weighed against the crippling effects of social anxiety, these slight, temporary disturbances are generally deemed quite acceptable by most patients.

HOW LONG

A reasonable question arises regarding the drugs discussed here: "How long will I have to take these medications?" The answer is, simply, we do not know. Most people treated with the medications alone tend to relapse after drugs are discontinued, though some—for reasons that are unclear—do not. This finding suggests that a combination, involving both drugs and cognitive behavioral therapy, is the treatment of choice to alleviate the life-restricting effects of social phobia. But in presenting options, a book can only describe the field. It is up to the individual clinician in cooperation with the patient to customize a treatment approach that will yield the most long-lasting results.

A FINAL WORD

It is clear that social anxiety has its roots in biology and is shaped by life experiences, and that extreme social anxiety is a matter of being oversensitive to the cues that trigger it. It is ironic that a mechanism that functions to allow human beings to coexist peacefully in groups can also cause such distress for some, becoming in effect too much of a good thing. But Sagan and Druyan have suggested a reason why the system that controls aggression to make group living possible may occasionally appear miscalibrated. "The evolutionary process has worked to achieve the right level of aggression—not too much, not too little—and the right inhibitors and disinhibitors," they write. "We emerge out of a turbulent mix of contradictory inclinations. It should be no surprise that in our psychology and our politics a similar tension of opposites apply."[11]

For those who suffer from social phobia, this new perspective on an old problem is good news. No longer is it appropriate to consider themselves "just shy" and go untreated. As our understanding clarifies and word of effective treatments spreads, more and more people whose lives have been limited and diminished by this disabling disorder are able to step forward with new confidence into the social world.

Appendix:
The Other Anxiety Disorders

I N THE OLD DAYS, before psychiatrists began to focus on anxiety itself, the conditions described as anxiety disorders used to be called psychoneuroses. Although several distinct disorders, each with its own set of symptoms, make up this group of conditions (see the accompanying table), all are marked by the sufferer's awareness that the symptoms are excessive or unreasonable. In this respect, the anxiety disorders are quite different from other mental disorders, such as schizophrenia or manic depressive illness, in which a person may lose contact with reality. Though the latter disorders are commonly considered major mental illnesses, the anxiety disorders can also be extraordinarily disabling. They do not proceed or "worsen" into other psychiatric conditions—except depression—but patients nevertheless often fear that they are "going crazy." The intensity of the anxiety symptoms may be matched only by the bewilderment accompanying the feeling that "I'm going crazy—and I don't know why."

Anxiety Disorders

- Panic Disorders with Agoraphobia
- Panic Disorders without Agoraphobia
- Social Phobia
- Simple Phobia
- Obsessive-Compulsive Disorder
- Post-Traumatic Stress Disorder
- Generalized Anxiety Disorder

PANIC DISORDER

The most common anxiety condition we see in our clinic is panic disorder. People with this condition suffer from unexpected, spontaneous attacks of symptoms that mix terror, an overwhelming sense of dread or of losing control, and physical symptoms such as palpitations, light-headedness, shortness of breath, chest pain, trembling, and weakness. These "fits" of panic instantly extinguish a sense of normality and make some patients believe that they are dying. Panic patients characteristically make frightened midnight visits to hospital emergency rooms and often present what we call the "thick-chart syndrome"—page after page in their medical records documenting visits to ten, twenty, or thirty medical specialists in the effort to track down and treat their "mysterious illnesses."

Because the physical manifestations of panic are often confusing and the sufferers are generally convinced that "something is wrong—I feel that I'm dying," this condition can be very expensive. Thousands of dollars' worth of medical tests often precede referral to our clinic. In the past, when the appropriate physical symptoms were ruled out, doctors tended to dismiss the patient, saying, "There's nothing wrong with you" or "It's all in your mind." Much of our work as anxiety specialists over the 1980s and 1990s has consisted of training other medical personnel, and especially emergency room physicians, in recognizing and treating the symptoms of panic disorder.

Many people with panic disorder develop avoidance behaviors, collectively referred to as agoraphobia, in response to their attacks. Because of the fear of having a panic attack, the list of places or situations to be avoided can grow to include wide-open areas, closed areas such as elevators, shopping malls, theaters, concerts, public transportation, being alone, and anywhere where there might be a crowd or the necessity of standing in line. For the agoraphobic, all these situations take on a quality of danger, of being "unsafe," and increasingly the avoidance restricts the sufferer's activities. Not surprisingly, many agoraphobics are homebound, unable to work, and often completely dependent on others.

One middle-aged woman traced her agoraphobia to three panic attacks she suffered in college. By the time I met her—on a house call—she had not crossed the threshold of her house for twenty years. On the other hand, some patients do leave home but can only move in certain circumscribed patterns within certain boundaries. Streets or highways mark the edges of their "safe" worlds—and they gradually stop even considering the possibility of stepping beyond those boundaries.

It is from research into panic disorder that we are beginning to learn about the physiological manifestations of the human "alarm system." It has been hypothesized that panic of this sort results from a hypersensitivity or lowered threshold in the locus ceruleus. This small area in the brain appears to trigger fear and its accompanying physical symptoms, although the phenomenon is much more complex than this.

Agoraphobic fears probably have an evolutionary significance. Chapter 2 discussed speculations regarding the evolutionary function of anxiety: in the developing human species, fears of being alone, too far from home, or trapped in various situations could well have served to protect vulnerable *homo sapiens* from predators or other physical dangers.

It was not until psychiatry began to focus on anxiety as a phenomenon in its own right that we began to find ways of treating panic attacks. Before coming to our anxiety clinic, many patients had gone through (and paid for) thousands of hours of "talking therapy" to little or no effect. I found it tremendously gratifying to learn, with many of the rest of the psychiatric community, that these devastating conditions were not only responsive to medical treatments and more specific interventions, but actually relatively easy to treat and control.

OBSESSIVE-COMPULSIVE DISORDER

Perhaps the most mysterious of the anxiety disorders is obsessive-compulsive disorder, made familiar but no less awesome by Judith Rapoport's popular book *The Boy Who Couldn't Stop Washing*.[1] With this disorder, patients' lives are dominated by obsessional thoughts, often about disease, contamination, fear of harming others, inexplicable concerns about asymmetries, and so on. Compulsions—subjective urges to repeat meaningless rituals such as excessive hand washing, cleaning, repeated checking (of lights, stoves, windows, appliances, and so on)—complete the pattern, and substantial anxiety arises if the obsessive-compulsive patient is blocked from completing these behaviors. Full-blown obsessive-compulsive disorder can be disabling simply by virtue of absorbing every waking minute with obsessional thoughts and rituals.

Although the underlying patterns of obsessive-compulsive disorder remain virtually the same, the rituals and fears that such patients describe are remarkably diverse. Some are only able to do things in certain numbered sequences; others count and recount certain objects, or touch walls or objects a certain number of times. While the meaning of the rituals remains mysterious, even for the sufferer, the forms they take are fascinating. One young man bore the terrible burden of having to repeat thoughts in certain sequences so the world would not end.

Another counted to specific numbers to guarantee the safety of loved ones. Still another, grappling with a fear of contamination, washed her hands twenty to fifty times a day, causing painfully cracked skin and bleeding. So fierce was another patient's fear of germs and disease that she actually managed, for fifteen years, to require that her husband and children wash their hands and feet in Lysol every time they entered the house. Many other patients suffered similar overwhelming fears of contamination from a variety of pollutants—gas, oil, HIV or AIDS viruses, or "radioactive materials."

A number of patients over the years were hoarders, who filled up their apartments or homes with all the materials that the rest of us would throw away—including garbage, feces, and so on—driven by a fear that something terrible would happen if they let anything go.

Another theme expressed by obsessive-compulsive patients is the fear of harming others. One man was afraid that he was about to confess that he had murdered someone, and all his energies, all his attentions, went to preventing this strange and groundless confession. Another constantly circled the block in his car to be sure he had not hit anyone—and then had to re-circle to confirm that the disaster had not happened during his subsequent trip or escaped his notice the first time. With his attention constantly pinned on the cycle before, he was in danger of driving round and round anxiously forever. A variation on this theme was particularly distressing and bizarre—a man who rode a bicycle everywhere was unable to keep himself from looking over his shoulder after he had passed a woman on the street. He was constantly attempting to reassure himself that he had not attacked and raped the woman he had passed.

Obsessive-compulsive disorder is another condition that had been only marginally treatable in the past. But with the new research on anxiety during the 1980s—biological investigation with an emphasis on finding effective medication, new technologies such as magnetic resonance imaging and positron emission tomography, and explanations of neurochemical, neuroanatomical, and genetic factors—rapid developments in understanding have led to exciting and effective therapies. With the combination of drug treatment and other approaches, patients who could have spent their entire lifetimes imprisoned by their obsession and compulsions have been able to break free, to lead normal lives.

POST-TRAUMATIC STRESS DISORDER

The Vietnam War and the escalating violence in American society have given us a living laboratory in which to study the effects of trauma. The victims of war and crime flooding our cities and public agencies since the 1970s corresponded with our new interest in and sensitivity to anxiety conditions. Careful research into the effects of the extremes of human trauma—for example, rape, assault, and injuries and losses of war—led to the definition of yet another anxiety condition: post-traumatic stress disorder. Patients with this condition suffer sleep disturbances, withdrawal and distancing from others, behavioral changes such as explosive outbursts, alcohol or drug abuse, antisocial behavior and law breaking, depression and a preoccupation with suicide, and a host of assorted nonspecific physical complaints.

Constant flashbacks to the trauma and its context are prominent, often triggered by sensory reminders. For example, many Vietnam veterans are assailed by highly detailed images of war at the sound of helicopter blades. One veteran left a bar with his friend and found himself in a street scene reminiscent of the many nights he had spent in Saigon. Suddenly, after a minor argument, the distinctions between past and present blurred, and he drew the pistol he had carried everywhere since the war and shot the friend who accompanied him.

Some progress has been made in finding effective treatment for this condition, but post-traumatic stress disorder remains difficult to treat.

SIMPLE PHOBIAS

"A phobia is a persistent, excessive, and unreasonable fear of a circumscribed stimulus (object, activity, or situation) that leads an individual to avoid the stimulus." So reads the *Diagnosis and Treatment of Anxiety Disorders: A Physician's Handbook.*[2] This rather bland description obscures the fierce grip such terrors—for example, of heights, snakes, spiders, rodents, dogs—have on phobia sufferers. One woman was so intensely afraid of encountering vermin such as mice and spiders that she never left her town. The fears rose up only in response to the presence of these creatures, so by carefully circumscribing her life, she was able to control them. But another source of suffering assailed her: her parents in Florida were ailing and probably dying, and she was unable to garner the courage to board a plane and fly to them. All she could think about when she managed to focus on the prospect was the array of small creatures she was liable to see were she actually to travel to a warm state.

As with the other anxiety disorders, our experience over the 1970s and 1980s has given us more insight into the mechanisms behind phobias and offered effective treatments and cures, largely techniques of exposure and desensitization.

GENERALIZED ANXIETY DISORDER

The chief symptom of general anxiety disorder (GAD) is a continuous stream of anxious thoughts. There are no discrete attacks or episodes of anxiety, as with panic disorder; rather, the patient experiences a persistent level of chronic anxiety that is unrelated to any other mental disorder. Family doctors often diagnose generalized anxiety disorder when patients present an unending string of hypochondriacal symptoms. To meet the criteria for GAD, one's anxious mood must have persisted for at least six months. "It's gotten to the point where it's the *worry* about my taxes that is the worst part. I'm thinking about them all the time, driving myself crazy with this in March and April—and then something else pops up to freak me out." This is a typical statement by someone with this diffuse anxiety disorder. The concerns might seem realistic enough to an outsider, and indeed they usually do have some basis in reality. It is the excessive, persistent nature that distinguishes this form of anxiety from the normal cares and concerns of life. In addition, patients with GAD experience a variety of physical symptoms, such as shortness of breath, palpitations, dizziness, sweating, flushing, dry mouth, frequent urination, nausea, and muscle tension. Headaches, abdominal complaints, and drug and alcohol abuse are all common in patients diagnosed with GAD. Some psychiatrists are beginning to believe that GAD may be a chronic or altered form of panic disorder.

Notes

PROLOGUE. THE DISORDERS OF THE DECADE

1. American Psychiatric Association, *Diagnostic and Statistical Manual of Mental Disorders*, 3d rev. ed. (Washington, D.C.: American Psychiatric Association, 1987).

2. J. K. Meyer, M. M. Weissman, G. L. Tischler, C. E. Holzer, P. J. Leaf, H. Orvaschel, J. C. Anthony, J. H. Boyd, J. D. Burke, M. Kramer, and R. Stolzman, "Six-month Prevalence of Psychiatric Disorders in Three Communities: 1980 to 1982," *Archives of General Psychiatry* 41 (1984): 959–66.

3. R. A. Schurman, P. S. Kramer, and J. B. Mitchell, "The Hidden Mental Health Network: Treatment of Mental Illness by Non-Psychiatric Physicians," *Archives of General Psychiatry* 42 (1985): 89–94.

4. W. Katon, P. P. Bitaliano, J. Russo, L. Cormier, K. Anderson, and M. Jones, "Panic Disorder: Epidemiology and Primary Care," *Journal of Family Practice* 23 (1986): 233–39.

CHAPTER 1. BURIED SECRETS/BURIED LIVES: TWO CASE HISTORIES

1. American Psychiatric Association, *Diagnostic and Statistical Manual of Mental Disorders*, 3d rev. ed. (Washington, D.C.: American

Psychiatric Association, 1987), p. 243.

2. M. R. Liebowitz, J. M. Gorman, A. J. Fyer, D. F. Klein, "Social Phobia: Review of a Neglected Anxiety Disorder," *Archives of General Psychiatry* 42 (1985): 729–35.

CHAPTER 2. THE EVOLUTIONARY ORIGINS OF SOCIAL ANXIETY

1. M. Chance, "An Ethnological Assessment of Emotion," in *Emotion, Theory, Research and Experience, vol. I,* ed. R. Plutchik and H. Kellerman (New York: Academic Press, 1980); P. Gilbert, *Human Nature and Suffering* (New York: Guilford Press, 1992).

2. Gilbert, *Human Nature and Suffering.*

3. Arne Öhman, "Face the Beast and Fear the Face: Animal and Social Fears as Prototypes for Evolutionary Analyses of Emotion," *Psychophysiology* 23, no. 2 (1986): 123–45; Peter Trower, Paul Gilbert, and Georgina Sherling, "Social Anxiety, Evolution, and Self-Presentation," in *The Handbook of Social and Evaluation Anxiety,* ed. Harold Leitenberg (New York: Plenum Press, 1990), pp. 11–45; Carl Sagan and Ann Druyan, *Shadows of Forgotten Ancestors: The Search for Who We Are* (New York: Random House, 1992).

4. E. Hoffman, *Relations in Public: Micro-Studies of the Public Order* (Middlesex: Penguin, 1972).

5. Sagan and Druyan, *Shadows of Forgotten Ancestors,* p. 216.

6. J. Hokanson and R. Edelman, "The Effects of Three Social Responses on Vascular Processes," *Journal of Personality and Social Psychology* 3, no. 4 (1966): 442–47.

CHAPTER 3. THE DRAMA OF SOCIAL PHOBIA

1. P. L. Amies, M. G. Gelder, and P. M. Shaw, "Social Phobia: A Comparative Clinical Study," *British Journal of Psychiatry* 142 (1983): 174–79.

2. T. W. Uhde, M. E. Tancer, B. Black, and T. M. Brown, "Phenomenology and Neurobiology of Social Phobia: Comparison with

Panic Disorder," *Journal of Clinical Psychology* 52 (November 1991): 31–40.

3. G. A. Pollard and J. G. Hendersen, "Four Types of Social Phobia in a Community Sample," *Journal of Nervous and Mental Disorders* 76 (1988): 440–45.

4. G. Williams and E. Degernhardt, "Paruresis: A Survey of a Disorder of a Micturition," *Journal of General Psychology* 51 (1929): 2954; D. L. Gruber and D. R. Shupe, "Personality Correlates of Urinary Hesitancy (Paruresis) and Body Shyness in Male College Students," *Journal of College Student Personnel* 23 (July 1982): 308–13; G. D. Zgouriedes, "Paruresis: Overview and Implications for Treatment," *Psychology Reports* 60 (1987): 1171–76.

5. Uhde, Tancer, Black, and Brown, "Phenomenology and Neurobiology"; Pollard and Hendersen, "Four Types of Social Phobia."

6. J. Cheek, *Conquering Shyness* (New York: Dell Publishing, 1989).

CHAPTER 4. JOINING THE GROUP
AT SCHOOL AND WORK

1. P. G. Freidman, *Shyness and Reticence in Students* (Washington, D.C.: National Educational Association, 1980).

2. S. M. Turner, D. C. Beidel, C. V. Dancu, and D. J. Keys, "Psychopathology of Social Phobia and Comparison to Avoidant Personality Disorder," *Journal of Abnormal Psychology* 95 (1986): 389–94.

3. A. Caspi, G. H. Elder, Jr., and D. J. Bem, "Moving Away from the World: Life-Course Patterns of Shy Children," *Developmental Psychology* 24 (1988): 824–31.

4. Carl Sagan and Ann Druyan, *Shadows of Forgotten Ancestors: The Search for Who We Are* (New York: Random House, 1992), p. 369.

5. J. R. T. Davidson, S. M. Ford, R. D. Smith, and N. L. S. Potts, "Long-term Treatment of Social Phobia Clonazepam," *Journal of Clinical Psychiatry* 52, no. 11 (1991 suppl.): 16–20.

6. Turner, Beidel, Dancu, and Keys, "Psychopathology of Social Phobia," p. 391.

7. P. G. Zimbardo, "Shyness and the Stresses of the Human Connection," *Handbook of Stress: Theoretical and Clinical Aspects*, ed. L. Golberger and S. Breznitz (New York: Free Press, 1982); P. G.

Zimbardo, *The Stanford Shyness Project: Shyness; Perspectives on Research and Treatment* (New York: Plenum Press, 1986).

CHAPTER 5. SOCIAL AND SEXUAL INTIMACY

1. J. M. Cheek and C. M. Busch, "The Influence of Shyness on Loneliness in a New Situation," *Personality and Social Psychology Bulletin* 7 (1981): 572–77; W. H. Jones, J. . Freeman, and R. A. Goswick, "The Persistence of Loneliness: Self and Other Determinants," *Journal of Personality* 49 (1981): 27–48;   W. H. Jones, J. Rose, and D. Russell, "Loneliness and Social Anxiety," in *Handbook of Social Evaluation Anxiety*, ed. H. Leitenberg (New York: Plenum Press, 1990), pp. 247–66.

2. L. S. Radloff, "Preventing the Harmful Consequences of Severe and Persistent Loneliness," Proceedings of a Research Planning Workshop, University of California, Los Angeles, February 10–12, 1982, National Institutes of Mental Health, Rockville, Md.; N. Bradburn, *The Structure of Psychological Well-Being* (Chicago: Aldine, 1989).

3. R. S. Weiss, *Loneliness: The Experience of Emotional and Social Isolation* (Cambridge, Mass.: MIT Press, 1973), p. 15.

4. M. R. Kundo, "Visual Literacy: Teaching Non-Verbal Communication through Television," *Educational Technology* 8 (1976): 31–33; J. Fast, *The Body Language of Sex, Power, and Aggression* (New York: Evans, 1977). The 65 percent figure is cited by Kundo; "honest language" is from Fast.

5. Virginia Satir, *Making Contact* (Millbrae, Calif.: Celestial Arts, 1976).

6. J. Ruesch, *Semiotic Approaches to Human Relations* (Paris: Moulton, 1972).

7. A. Kenden and A. Ferber, "A Description of Some Human Greetings," in *Comparative Ecology and Behavior of Primates*, ed. M. Michael and J. H. Cook (London: Academic Press, 1973), pp. 591–668.

8. Ibid.; I. Eibl-Eibesfeldt, "Similarities and Differences between Cultures and Expressive Movements," in *Nonverbal Communication*, ed. R. A. Hinde (Cambridge: Cambridge University Press, 1972), pp. 92–101.

9. Helen Fisher, *Anatomy of Love* (New York: Norton, 1992), pp.

19–20.

10. Ibid., pp. 21–23.

11. Ibid., pp. 26, 27–28.

12. Ibid., p. 28.

13. Ibid., p. 29.

14. W. H. Jones and B. N. Carpenter, "Shyness, Social Behavior, and Relationships," in *Shyness: Perspectives on Research and Treatment*, ed. W. H. Jones, J. M. Cheek, and S. R. Briggs (New York: Plenum Press, 1986), pp. 229–38.

15. S. L. Bem, "The Measurement of Psychological Androgyny," *Journal of Consulting and Clinical Psychology* 42 (1974): 155–62.

16. Fisher, *Anatomy of Love*, p. 32. See also T. Perper, *Sex Signals: The Biology of Love* (Philadelphia: ISI Press, 1985), and D. B. Givens, *Love Signals: How to Attract a Mate* (New York: Crown, 1983).

17. Quoted in Fisher, *Anatomy of Love*, p. 27.

18. Ibid., p. 21.

19. M. R. Leary and S. E. Dobbins, "Social Anxiety, Sexual Behavior, and Contraceptive Use," *Journal of Personality and Social Psychiatry* 43 (1983): 1347–54.

20. P. G. Zimbardo, *Shyness: What It Is, What to Do about It* (New York: Addison-Wesley, 1977), pp. 94–95.

21. Ibid., pp. 101–3.

22. J. G. Beck and D. H. Barlow, "Current Conceptualizations of Sexual Dysfunction: A Review and an Alternative Perspective," *Clinical Psychology Review* 4 (1984): 363–78.

23. W. Masters and V. Johnson, *Human Sexual Inadequacy* (Boston: Little, Brown, 1970).

24. P. L. Amies, M. G. Gelder, and P. M. Shaw, "Social Phobia: A Comparative Clinical Study," *British Journal of Psychiatry* 142 (1983): 174–79; G. Persson, and C. M. Norlund, "Agoraphobics and Social Phobics: Differences in Background Factors, Syndrome Profiles, and Therapeutic Response, *Acta Psychiatry Scandinavia* (1985): 148–59; L. Solyom, B. Ledwidge, and C. Solyom, "Delineating Social Phobia," *British Journal of Psychiatry* 149 (1986): 464–70.

25. H. G. Gough and A. Thorne, "Positive, Negative, and Balanced Shyness: Self-Definitions and the Reactions of Others," in *Shyness: Perspectives on Research and Treatment*, ed. W. H. Jones, J. M. Cheek, and

S. R. Briggs (New York: Plenum Press, 1986).

26. A. Caspi, G. H. Elder, Jr., and D. J. Bem, "Moving Away from the World: Life-Course Patterns of Shy Children," *Developmental Psychology* 24 (1988): 824–31.

CHAPTER 6. SOCIAL FEAR IN CHILDREN

1. R. A. Spitz, *The First _ ar of Life* (New York: International Universities Press, 1965).

2. J. Bowlby, *Attachment and Loss,* vol. 1, *Attachment* (London: Hogarth, 1969); J. Bowlby, *Attachment and Loss,* vol. 2, *Separation* (London: Hogarth, 1973).

3. I. M. Marks, *Fears, Phobias, and Rituals: Panic, Anxiety and Their Disorders* (Oxford: Oxford University Press, 1987).

4. A. H. Buss, *Self-Consciousness and Social Anxiety* (San Francisco: Freeman, 1980).

5. H. Campbell, "Morbid Shyness," *British Medical Journal* 2 (1986): 805–7.

6. P. G. Zimbardo, *Shyness: What It Is and What to Do about It* (New York: Addison-Wesley, 1977); P. G. Zimbardo and S. L. Radl, *The Shy Child* (New York: McGraw-Hill, 1981). See also M. Girardo, *Shy? You Don't Have to Be!* (New York: Pocket Books, 1978); G. M. Phillips, *Help for Shy People* (Englewood Cliffs, N.J.: Prentice-Hall, 1981).

7. P. G. Zimbardo, "Shyness and the Stresses of the Human Connection," in *Handbook of Stress: Theoretical and Clinical Aspects,* ed. L. Goldberger and S. Breznitz (New York: Free Press, 1982), pp. 471–73; P. G. Zimbardo, P. A. Pilkonis, and R. Norwood, "The Social Disease Called Shyness," *Psychology Today* 8 (1975): 68–72; P. G. Zimbardo, *The Stanford Shyness Project: Perspectives on Research and Treatment* (New York: Plenum Press, 1986).

8. Zimbardo, *The Stanford Shyness Project;* P. A. Pilkonis, "The Behavioral Consequences of Shyness," *Journal of Personality* 45 (1977): 596–611.

9. Zimbardo, "Shyness and Stresses of the Human Connection," p. 478.

10. American Psychiatric Association, *Diagnostic and Statistical Manual of Mental Disorders,* 3d ed. rev. (Washington, D.C.: American

Psychiatric Association, 1987), pp. 58–65.

11. C. G. Last and C. C. Straus, "School Refusal and Anxiety-Disordered Children and Adolescence," *Journal of the American Academy of Childhood and Adolescent Psychology* 29 (1990): 31–35.

12. J. Kagan and H. A. Moss, *Birth to Maturity* (New Haven: Yale University Press, 1983).

13. J. Kagan, J. S. Resnik, and N. Snidman, "Biological Bases of Childhood Shyness," *Science* 8 (1988): 167–71; J. Kagan, J. S. Resnik, N. Snidman, J. Gibbons, and M. O. Johnson, "Childhood Derivatives of Inhibition and Lack of Inhibition to the Unfamiliar," *Child Development* 59 (1988): 1580–89.

14. Kagan's findings are in Kagan et al., "Childhood Derivatives of Inhibition."

15. Kagan, Resnik, and Snidman, "Biological Bases of Childhood Shyness"; Kagan et al., "Childhood Derivatives of Inhibition."

16. R. Plomin and D. Daniels, "Genetics and Shyness," in *Shyness: Perspectives on Research and Treatment*, ed. W. H. Jones,   J. M. Cheek, and S. R. Briggs (New York: Plenum Press, 1986).

17. A. H. Buss, "A Theory of Shyness," in *Shyness: Perspectives on Research and Treatment*, ed. W. H. Jones, J. M. Cheek, and S. R. Briggs (New York: Plenum Press, 1986).

18. G. Parker, "Reported Parental Characteristics of Agoraphobics and Social Phobics," *British Journal of Psychiatry* 155 (1979): 555–60.

19. S. R. Briggs and L. M. Cheadle, "Retrospective Accounts of the Development of Shyness," Paper presented at the Southwestern Psychological Association, Fort Worth, Texas, 1986.

20. I. R. Bell, M. L. Jasnoski, J. Kagan, and D. King, "Is Allergic Rhinitis More Frequent in Young Adults with Extreme Shyness? A Preliminary Survey," *Psychosomatic Medicine* 52 (1990): 517–25.

21. W. H. Jones, J. M. Cheek, and S. R. Briggs, eds., *Shyness: Perspectives on Research and Treatment* (New York: Plenum Press, 1986), pp. 91–103.

CHAPTER 7. SEEING . . . AND BEING SEEN

1. E. D. Blest, "Function of Eye Spot Patterns in a Lepidoptera," *Behavior* 11 (1957): 120–54.

2.   Patricia Webbink, *The Power of the Eyes* (New York: Springer, 1986).

3.   D. Howes, "A Word Count of Spoken English," *Journal of Verbal Learning and Verbal Behavior* 5 (1966): 572–604.

4.   G. Schaller, *The Mountain Gorilla: Ecology and Behavior* (Chicago: University of Chicago Press, 1963).

5.   H. Scheinfield, cited in D. G. Freedman, *Human Social Biology: A Holistic Approach* (New York: Free Press, 1979).

6.   P. C. Ellsworth, J. M. Carlsmith, and A. Henson, "The Stare as a Stimulus to Flight and Human Subjects: A Series of Field Experiments," *Journal of Personality and Social Psychology* 21 (1992): 302–11; P. C. Ellsworth, "Direct Gaze as a Social Stimulus: The Example of Aggression," in *Nonverbal Communication of Aggression*, ed. P. Pliner, L. Krames, and T. Alloway (New York: Plenum Press, 1975), pp. 53–76.

7.   C. L. Kleinke, *First Impressions: The Psychology of Encountering Others* (Englewood Cliffs, N.J.: Prentice-Hall, 1975).

8.   P. Ekman, *Telling Lies: Clues to Deceit in the Marketplace, Politics and Marriage* (New York: Norton, 1992).

9.   P. Ekman and W. V. Friesen, *Unmasking the Face* (Englewood Cliffs, N.J.: Prentice-Hall, 1975).

10.   M. Argyle, "Eye Contact," in *Basic Readings in Communication Theory*, ed. C. C. Mortenson (New York: Harper and Row, 1973).

11.   R. B. Exline and D. Messick, "The Effects of Dependency and Social Reinforcement upon Visual Behavior during an Interview," *British Journal of Social and Clinical Psychology* 6 (1967): 256–66.

12.   P. Ekman and W. V. Friesen, "Nonverbal Leakage and Clues to Deception," *Psychiatry* 32 (1969): 88–106.

13.   M. Argyle, *Body Communication* (London: Methven, 1975).

14.   D. R. Buchanan, M. Goldman, and R. Juhnke, "Eye Contact, Sex, and the Violation of Personal Space," *Journal of Social Psychology* 103 (1977): 19–25.

15.   P. C. Ellsworth, "Direct Gaze as a Stimulus for Aggression," in *Nonverbal Communication of Aggression*, ed. P. Pliner, L. Krames, and T. Alloway (New York: Plenum Press, 1975), pp. 53–76.

16.   Ibid.

17.   P. L. Amies, M. G. Gelder, and P. M. Shaw, "Social Phobia: A Comparative Clinical Study," *British Journal of Psychiatry* 142 (1983):

174–79.

18. T. Williams, *Memoirs* (New York: Doubleday, 1976), p. 12.

19. C. Darwin, *The Expression of the Emotions in Man and in Animals* (Chicago and London: Chicago Press, 1965), pp. 309–46.

20. Ibid., p. 326.

21. R. J. Edelmann, *The Psychology of Embarrassment* (New York: John Wiley and Sons, 1987), p. 71.

22. J. Rodin, *Body Traps* (New York: William Morrow, 1992), p. 27.

23. W. E. Liebman and J. M. Cheek, "Shyness and Body Image," Paper presented at the annual meeting of the American Psychological Association, Anaheim, California, August 30, 1983.

24. W. H. Jones and D. Russell, "The Social Reticence Scale: An Objective Instrument to Measure Shyness," *Journal of Personality Assessment* 46 (1982): 629–31.

25. I. Marks and J. Mishan, "Dysmorphophobia Avoidance with Disturbed Bodily Perception: A Pilot Study of Exposure Therapy," *British Journal of Psychiatry* 152 (1988): 674–78.

26. M. B. Stein, I. J. Heuser, J. L. Juncos, and T. W. Uhde, "Anxiety Disorders in Patients with Parkinsons Disease," *American Journal of Psychiatry* 147 (1992): 217–20.

CHAPTER 8. TREMBLING IN THE WINGS

1. Stephen Aaron, *Stage Fright: Its Role in Acting* (Chicago: University of Chicago Press, 1986), pp. 59, 62.

2. Lawrence Olivier, *Confessions of an Actor: An Autobiography* (New York: Simon and Schuster, 1982), pp. 261–62; Aaron, *Stage Fright*, p. 61.

3. Michael Frank, "Rosalind Russell," *Architectural Digest* (April 1992): 190–91 and 276.

4. Aaron, *Stage Fright*, p. 60.

5. J. M. Corredor, *Conversations with Casals* (New York: Dutton, 1956), p. 29.

6. J. Hall, "After an Onstage Collapse and a Six-Year Battle with Stage Fright, Carly Simon Braves a Comeback," *People*, August 17, 1987, 38–40.

7. "Walter Scott's Personality Parade," *Parade: The Sunday*

Newspaper Magazine, November 21, 1993, 2.

8. J. Leo, "Take Me Out to the Ballgame," *Time*, August 15, 1983, 72.

9. Loren Feldman, "Strikeouts and Psych-Outs," *New York Times Magazine*, July 7, 1991, 10–13, 30.

10. Aaron, *Stage Fright*, back cover.

11. A. Steptoe and H. Fidler, "Stage Fright and Orchestral Musicians: A Study of Cognitive Behavioral Strategies and Performance Anxiety," *British Journal of Psychology* 78 (1987): 241–49.

12. R. B. Wesner, R. Noyes, Jr., and T. L. Davis, "The Occurrence of Performance Anxiety among Musicians," *Journal of Affective Disorders* 18 (1990): 177–85.

13. M. Fishbein, S. E. Middlestadt, V. Ottati, S. Straus, and A. Ellis, "Medical Problems among ICSOM," *Problems of Performing Artists* 3 (1988): 1–8.

14. Aaron, *Stage Fright*, p. 61.

15. P. Taggart, M. Carruthers, and W. Somerville, "Electrocardiogram, Plasma Catacholamines and Lipids, and Their Modification by Oxprenolol, When Speaking before an Audience," *Lancet*, August 18, 1973, 341–46.

16. Aaron, *Stage Fright*, pp. 60, 62.

17. P. G. Salmon, "A Psychological Perspective on Musical Performance Anxiety: A Review of the Literature," *Medical Problems of Performing Artists* (March 1990): 2–11.

18. Robert Moss, "Stage Fright Is Actors' Eternal Nemesis," *New York Times*, January 6, 1992, E2.

CHAPTER 9. SELF-MEDICATION WITH ALCOHOL AND DRUGS

1. M. G. Kushner, K. J. Sher, and B. D. Beitman, "The Relationship between Alcohol Problems and the Anxiety Disorders," *American Journal of Psychiatry* 6 (1990): 147; J. A. Mullany and C. J. Trippett, "Alcohol Dependence and Phobias: Clinical Description and Relevance," *British Journal of Psychology* 135 (1979): 565–73.

2. M. A. Schucket, "Genetic and Clinical Implications of Alcohol

and Affective Disorder," *American Journal of Psychiatry* 143 (1986): 140–47; P. Z. Amies, M. G. Gelder, and P. M. Shaw, "Social Phobia: A Comparative Clinical Study," *British Journal of Psychiatry* 142 (1983): 174–79; B. A. Thyer, R. T. Hinle, O. J. Cameron, G. C. Curtis, and R. M. Nesse, "Alcohol Abuse among Clinically Anxious Patients," *Behavioral Research and Therapy* 24 (1986): 389–94; S. M. Turner, D. C. Beidel, C. V. Dancu, and D. J. Keys, "Psychopathology of Social Phobia and Comparison to Avoidant Personality Disorder," *Journal of Abnormal Psychology* 95 (1986): 389–94. The 50 percent figure is cited by Turner.

3. F. R. Schneier, L. Y. Martin, M. R. Liebowitz, J. M. Gorman, and A. J. Fyer, "Alcohol Abuse and Social Phobia," *Journal of Anxiety Disorders* 3 (1989): 15–23.

4. P. G. Zimbardo, *Shyness* (New York: Addison-Wesley, 1977), p. 106, my emphasis.

5. R. M. Page, "Shyness as a Risk Factor for Adolescent Substance Abuse," *Journal of School Health* 59 (December 1989): 432–35.

6. Ibid., p. 434.

CHAPTER 10. DIAGNOSIS AND TREATMENT

1. M. Mannuzza, A. J. Fyer, M. R. Liebowitz, and D. F. Klein, "Delineating the Boundaries of Social Phobia: Its Relationship to Panic Disorder and Agoraphobia," *Journal of Anxiety Disorders* 4 (1990): 41–59.

2. J. R. T. Davidson, N. L. S. Potts, E. A. Richichi, S. M. Ford, K. R. R. Krishman, R. D. Smith, and W. Wilson, "The Brief Social Phobia Scale," *Journal of Clinical Psychiatry* 52, no. 11 (1991 suppl.): 48–51.

3. A. T. Beck, G. Emery, and R. Greenberg, *Anxiety Disorders and Phobia: A Cognitive Perspective* (New York: Guilford Press, 1985).

4. R. J. Heimberg, R. E. Becker, K. Goldfinger, and J. A. Vermilyea, "Treatment of Social Phobia by Exposure, Cognitive Restructuring, and Homework Assignments," *Journal of Nervous and Mental Disease* 173 (1985): 236–45.

5. P. D. Kramer, *Listening to Prozac* (New York: Viking, 1993).

6. C. Brantigan, T. Brantigan, and N. Joseph, "Effect of Beta-Blockade and Beta-Stimulation on Stage Fright," *American Journal of*

Medicine 72 (1982): 88–94; K. Neftel, R. Adler, L. Kappell, M. Rosi, M. Dolder, H. Kaser, H. Bruggesser, and H. Vorkauf, "Stage Fright in Musicians: A Model Illustrating the Effect of Beta-Blockers," *Psychosomatic Medicine* 44 (1982): 461–69.

7.   M. R. Liebowitz, E. M. Quitkin, J. W. Stewart, P. J. McGrath, W. M. Hanison, J. S. Markowitz, J. G. Rabkin, E. Tricamo, D. M. Goetz, and D. F. Klein, "Antidepressants Specificity in Atypical Depression," *Archives of General Psychiatry* 45 (1988): 129–37.

8.   M. R. Liebowitz, F. R. Schneier, E. Hollander, L. A. Welkowitz, J. B. Saoud, J. Feerick, R. Campeas, B. A. Fallon, L. Street, and A. Gitow, "Treatment of Social Phobia with Drugs Other Than Benzodiazepines," *Journal of Clinical Psychiatry* 52 (1991 suppl.): 10–15.

9.   J. A. Deltito and M. Stam, "Psychopharmacological Treatment of Avoidant Personality Disorder," *Comprehensive Psychiatry* 30 (1989): 498–504; F. R. Schneier, S. J. Chin, E. Hollander, and M. R. Liebowitz, "Fluoxetine in Social Phobia," letter to the editor, *Journal of Clinical Psychopharmacology* 12 (1992): 62–63.

10.   J. R. T. Davidson, S. M. Ford, R. D. Smith, and N. L. S. Potts, "Long-Term Treatment of Social Phobia with Clonazepam," *Journal of Clinical Psychiatry* 52, no. 11 (1991 suppl.): 16–20.

11.   Carl Sagan and Ann Druyan, *Shadows of Forgotten Ancestors: The Search for Who We Are* (New York: Random House, 1992), p. 200.

APPENDIX. THE OTHER ANXIETY DISORDERS

1.   Judith L. Rapoport, *The Boy Who Couldn't Stop Washing* (New York: Penguin, 1991).

2.   T. J. McGlynn and H. L. Metcalf, *Diagnosis and Treatment of Anxiety Disorders: A Physician's Handbook* (New York: American Psychiatric Press, 1989), p. 87.

Index